KETO DIET

Book For Beginners 2023

1800 Easy & Healthy Effortless Recipes with 28-Day Meal Plan with Low Carb to Lose Weight

Sienna Fowler

CONTENTS

SOUPS, STEW & SALADS RECIPES 60

DESSERTS AND DRINKS RECIPES...71

APPENDIX : RECIPES INDEX 81

INTRODUCTION

In the realm of health-focused gastronomy, Sienna stands out as a trailblazer, intertwining the science of nutritional ketosis with the art of creating palatable masterpieces.

Sienna Fowler knows first-hand the life-changing potential of the Keto diet. Her personal journey towards health and wellness sparked the creation of this comprehensive cookbook. Each recipe is a product of her own experiences, dedication, and a relentless pursuit to make the Keto lifestyle accessible, enjoyable, and incredibly tasty.

This cookbook transcends the conventional. It is not merely a collection of recipes, but an inviting narrative into Sienna's kitchen, where she marries nutritional science with culinary creativity. With her curated selection of 1800 delectable recipes and a 28-day meal plan, Sienna offers a practical and joyous roadmap to navigate the Keto diet with finesse.

As you flip through these pages, you will uncover more than just a guide to low-carb, high-fat meals. You'll encounter tales of determination, innovation, and passion. Each recipe encapsulates Sienna's journey of turning dietary constraints into culinary triumphs, and her unwavering belief that healthy eating can still be indulgent and satisfying.

Step into Sienna Fowler's culinary world, where you'll find a balance between nutrient-rich meals and exquisite flavors, and every dish is a testament to the rewarding Keto lifestyle. Welcome to a transformative food journey.

What are the main features of the Keto Diet?

High in Healthy Fats

The diet involves consuming about 70-75% of your daily calories from healthy fats. Sources can include avocados, olive oil, coconut oil, butter, and fatty cuts of meat. This high fat intake is what puts your body into a state of ketosis, where it begins to burn fat for energy instead of carbohydrates.

Low in Carbohydrates

Only about 5-10% of your daily calories should come from carbs on a ketogenic diet. That's about 20-50 grams of carbs per day, depending on your caloric needs. High-carb foods like grains, starchy vegetables, legumes, and fruits are generally limited, with a focus on low-carb vegetables like leafy greens instead.

Moderate Protein Intake

Protein intake should be moderate, making up about 20% of daily calories. Overconsumption of protein can prevent the body from entering ketosis because excess protein can be converted into glucose.

Ketosis

The goal of the diet is to reach a metabolic state called ketosis, where the body is burning fat for energy instead of carbohydrates. This can result in weight loss and increased energy levels.

What are the potential long-term health effects of a Keto Diet?

• Improved Weight Management

The ketogenic diet can help individuals maintain a healthy weight over time, especially when paired with a sustainable, health-focused lifestyle.

• Enhanced Blood Sugar Control

The diet may be beneficial for individuals with type 2 diabetes by helping to improve insulin sensitivity and reduce blood sugar levels. Some people have been able to reduce or even discontinue their diabetes medications with the guidance of a healthcare professional.

• Heart Health

Some studies have shown improvements in certain cardiovascular risk factors, such as HDL cholesterol levels, blood pressure, and triglycerides. However, the impact on LDL cholesterol can vary, with some people experiencing elevated levels.

- **Brain Health**

There's emerging research suggesting the ketogenic diet may have neuroprotective effects. The diet has been used for almost a century to treat drug-resistant epilepsy, and recent studies are exploring its potential benefits for neurodegenerative conditions like Alzheimer's and Parkinson's disease.

- **Reduced Inflammation**

Some studies indicate that the ketogenic diet can reduce systemic inflammation, which is implicated in many chronic diseases.

- **Improved Energy and Mental Clarity**

Some adherents report sustained energy levels and increased mental clarity and focus, which could be attributed to the stable blood sugar levels maintained on the diet.

Questions you may care about this Keto Diet Cookbook

Q: Is this cookbook suitable for beginners with no knowledge of the Keto Diet?

Answer: Absolutely! This cookbook was designed with both beginners and experienced keto dieters in mind. It starts with an introductory section covering the basics of the Keto Diet, its principles and benefits, ensuring a solid foundation before delving into the recipes.

Q: Are the ingredients used in the recipe readily available?

Answer: Every effort has been made to ensure that most of the ingredients can be found at your local grocery store. The selected ingredients are common in daily life, try to meet the needs of novices as much as possible, and at the same time ensure that the food cooked is delicious and healthy

Q: I am vegetarian. Does this cookbook offer vegan Keto recipes?

Answer: Yes! The cookbook contains a variety of recipes for different dietary needs, many of which are suitable for vegetarians. Each vegetarian recipe is clearly labeled for easy identification.

Q: How diverse are the recipes? I worry about getting bored with repeated meals.

Answer: This cookbook offers a wide range of dishes, from breakfasts, main courses, and sides to desserts and snacks. With hundreds of recipes covering every cuisine and palate, mealtime is rarely monotonous.

Q: Is there a meal plan or guide for combining recipes for optimal Keto benefits?

Answer: Yes, this recipe includes a section dedicated to meal planning. This will guide you on how to combine recipes for a balanced ketogenic diet to ensure you achieve and maintain a state of ketosis while enjoying a variety of delicious meals.

28-Day Meal Plan

Day	Breakfast	Lunch	Dinner
1	Parmesan Crackers 7	Stewed Italian Chicken 16	Stewed Chicken Salsa 23
2	Parsnip And Carrot Fries With Aioli 8	Yummy Chicken Nuggets 16	Avocado And Tomato Burritos 59
3	Basil Keto Crackers 8	Habanero Chicken Wings 16	Lemon Cauliflower "couscous" With Halloumi 59
4	Choco And Coconut Bars 9	Chicken, Eggplant And Gruyere Gratin 17	Watermelon And Cucumber Salad 60
5	Coconut And Chocolate Bars 10	Turkey Fajitas 18	Traditional Greek Salad 60
6	Crab Stuffed Mushrooms 11	Spanish Chicken 18	Mushroom Soup 60
7	Balsamic Brussels Sprouts With Prosciutto 11	Chicken Breasts With Walnut Crust 19	Green Salad With Bacon And Blue Cheese 61
8	Keto-approved Trail Mix 12	Pesto Chicken 20	Arugula Prawn Salad With Mayo Dressing 61
9	Cajun Spiced Pecans 13	Herby Chicken Meatballs 21	Creamy Cauliflower Soup With Bacon Chips 62
10	Garlicky Cheddar Biscuits 13	Chicken, Broccoli & Cashew Stir-fry 21	Pumpkin & Meat Peanut Stew 62
11	Garlic And Basil Mashed Celeriac 14	Spinach Artichoke Heart Chicken 22	Beef Reuben Soup 63
12	Buttered Broccoli 14	Chicken Skewers With Celery Fries 22	Creamy Cauliflower Soup With Chorizo Sausage 63
13	Bacon And Chicken Cottage Pie 17	Chicken And Green Cabbage Casserole 23	Bacon Chowder 64
14	Pork Burgers With Caramelized Onion Rings 27	Stuffed Avocados With Chicken 23	Bacon And Pea Salad 64

Day	Breakfast	Lunch	Dinner
15	Homemade Classic Beef Burgers 30	One-pot Chicken With Mushrooms And Spinach 24	Filling Beefy Soup 31
16	Parmesan Roasted Cabbage 50	Chicken Breasts With Cheddar & Pepperoni 24	Shrimp With Avocado & Cauliflower Salad 64
17	Creamy Vegetable Stew 50	Cheesy Chicken Bake With Zucchini 25	Quail Eggs And Winter Melon Soup 65
18	Colorful Vegan Soup 51	Bacon Chicken Alfredo 25	Garlic Chicken Salad 65
19	Parsnip Chips With Avocado Dip 51	Thyme Chicken Thighs 26	Tuna Salad With Lettuce & Olives 65
20	Vegan Mushroom Pizza 52	Pork Chops With Cranberry Sauce 27	Mediterranean Salad 66
21	Creamy Kale And Mushrooms 52	Creamy Pork Chops 28	Green Salad 66
22	Zucchini Noodles 53	Russian Beef Gratin 28	Clam Chowder 66
23	Morning Coconut Smoothie 58	Grilled Lamb On Lemony Sauce 28	Brazilian Moqueca (shrimp Stew) 67
24	Coconut Cauliflower & Parsnip Soup 56	Spiced Baked Pork With Milk 29	Simplified French Onion Soup 67
25	Herbed Portobello Mushrooms 56	Caribbean Beef 29	Chicken And Cauliflower Rice Soup 68
26	Onion & Nuts Stuffed Mushrooms 57	Pork Osso Bucco 30	Grilled Steak Salad With Pickled Peppers 68
27	Strawberry Mug Cake 57	Beef With Dilled Yogurt 31	Kale And Brussels Sprouts 69
28	Pumpkin Bake 57	Beef Stuffed Roasted Squash 32	Asparagus Niçoise Salad 70

Measurement Conversions

BASIC KITCHEN CONVERSIONS & EQUIVALENTS

DRY MEASUREMENTS CONVERSION CHART

3 TEASPOONS = 1 TABLESPOON = 1/16 CUP

6 TEASPOONS = 2 TABLESPOONS = 1/8 CUP

12 TEASPOONS = 4 TABLESPOONS = 1/4 CUP

24 TEASPOONS = 8 TABLESPOONS = 1/2 CUP

36 TEASPOONS = 12 TABLESPOONS = 3/4 CUP

48 TEASPOONS = 16 TABLESPOONS = 1 CUP

METRIC TO US COOKING CONVERSIONS

OVEN TEMPERATURES

120 °C = 250 °F

160 °C = 320 °F

180° C = 350 °F

205 °C = 400 °F

220 °C = 425 °F

LIQUID MEASUREMENTS CONVERSION CHART

8 FLUID OUNCES = 1 CUP = 1/2 PINT = 1/4 QUART

16 FLUID OUNCES = 2 CUPS = 1 PINT = 1/2 QUART

32 FLUID OUNCES = 4 CUPS = 2 PINTS = 1 QUART

 = 1/4 GALLON

128 FLUID OUNCES = 16 CUPS = 8 PINTS = 4 QUARTS = 1 GALLON

BAKING IN GRAMS

1 CUP FLOUR = 140 GRAMS

1 CUP SUGAR = 150 GRAMS

1 CUP POWDERED SUGAR = 160 GRAMS

1 CUP HEAVY CREAM = 235 GRAMS

VOLUME

1 MILLILITER = 1/5 TEASPOON

5 ML = 1 TEASPOON

15 ML = 1 TABLESPOON

240 ML = 1 CUP OR 8 FLUID OUNCES

1 LITER = 34 FL. OUNCES

WEIGHT

1 GRAM = .035 OUNCES

100 GRAMS = 3.5 OUNCES

500 GRAMS = 1.1 POUNDS

1 KILOGRAM = 35 OUNCES

US TO METRIC COOKING CONVERSIONS

1/5 TSP = 1 ML

1 TSP = 5 ML

1 TBSP = 15 ML

1 FL OUNCE = 30 ML

1 CUP = 237 ML

1 PINT (2 CUPS) = 473 ML

1 QUART (4 CUPS) = .95 LITER

1 GALLON (16 CUPS) = 3.8 LITERS

1 OZ = 28 GRAMS

1 POUND = 454 GRAMS

BUTTER

1 CUP BUTTER = 2 STICKS = 8 OUNCES = 230 GRAMS = 8 TABLESPOONS

WHAT DOES 1 CUP EQUAL

1 CUP = 8 FLUID OUNCES

1 CUP = 16 TABLESPOONS

1 CUP = 48 TEASPOONS

1 CUP = 1/2 PINT

1 CUP = 1/4 QUART

1 CUP = 1/16 GALLON

1 CUP = 240 ML

BAKING PAN CONVERSIONS

1 CUP ALL-PURPOSE FLOUR = 4.5 OZ

1 CUP ROLLED OATS = 3 OZ 1 LARGE EGG = 1.7 OZ

1 CUP BUTTER = 8 OZ 1 CUP MILK = 8 OZ

1 CUP HEAVY CREAM = 8.4 OZ

1 CUP GRANULATED SUGAR = 7.1 OZ

1 CUP PACKED BROWN SUGAR = 7.75 OZ

1 CUP VEGETABLE OIL = 7.7 OZ

1 CUP UNSIFTED POWDERED SUGAR = 4.4 OZ

BAKING PAN CONVERSIONS

9-INCH ROUND CAKE PAN = 12 CUPS

10-INCH TUBE PAN =16 CUPS

11-INCH BUNDT PAN = 12 CUPS

9-INCH SPRINGFORM PAN = 10 CUPS

9 X 5 INCH LOAF PAN = 8 CUPS

9-INCH SQUARE PAN = 8 CUPS

Appetizers, Snacks & Side Dishes Recipes

Walnut Butter On Cracker

Servings: 1
Cooking Time: 0 Minutes
Ingredients:
- 1 tablespoon walnut butter
- 2 pieces Mary's gone crackers

Directions:
1. Spread ½ tablespoon of walnut butter per cracker and enjoy.

Nutrition Info:
- Info Per Servings 4.0g Carbs, 1.0g Protein, 14.0g Fat, 134 Calories

Buttery Herb Roasted Radishes

Servings: 6
Cooking Time: 25 Minutes
Ingredients:
- 2 lb small radishes, greens removed
- 3 tbsp olive oil
- Salt and black pepper to season
- 3 tbsp unsalted butter
- 1 tbsp chopped parsley
- 1 tbsp chopped tarragon

Directions:
1. Preheat oven to 400ºF and line a baking sheet with parchment paper. Toss radishes with oil, salt, and black pepper. Spread on baking sheet and roast for 20 minutes until browned.
2. Heat butter in a large skillet over medium heat to brown and attain a nutty aroma, 2 to 3 minutes.
3. Take out the parsnips from the oven and transfer to a serving plate. Pour over the browned butter atop and sprinkle with parsley and tarragon. Serve with roasted rosemary chicken.

Nutrition Info:
- Info Per Servings 2g Carbs, 5g Protein, 14g Fat, 160 Calories

Ricotta And Pomegranate

Servings: 3
Cooking Time: 12 Minutes
Ingredients:
- 1 cup Ricotta cheese
- 3 tablespoons olive oil
- 1/2 cup pomegranate Arils
- 2 tsp thyme, fresh
- 2 cups arugula leaves
- Pepper and salt to taste
- 1/2 tsp grated lemon zest

Directions:
1. Mix all ingredients in a bowl.
2. Toss until well combined.
3. Season with pepper and salt.
4. Serve and enjoy.

Nutrition Info:
- Info Per Servings 9g Carbs, 11g Protein, 25g Fat, 312 Calories

Parmesan Crackers

Servings: 6
Cooking Time: 25 Minutes
Ingredients:

- 1 ⅓ cups coconut flour
- 1 ¼ cup grated Parmesan cheese
- Salt and black pepper to taste
- 1 tsp garlic powder
- ⅓ cup butter, softened
- ⅓ tsp sweet paprika
- ⅓ cup heavy cream
- Water as needed

Directions:

1. Preheat the oven to 350ºF.
2. Mix the coconut flour, parmesan cheese, salt, pepper, garlic powder, and paprika in a bowl. Add in the butter and mix well. Top with the heavy cream and mix again until a smooth, thick mixture has formed. Add 1 to 2 tablespoon of water at this point, if it is too thick.
3. Place the dough on a cutting board and cover with plastic wrap. Use a rolling pin to spread out the dough into a light rectangle. Cut cracker squares out of the dough and arrange them on a baking sheet without overlapping. Bake for 20 minutes and transfer to a serving bowl after.

Nutrition Info:

- Info Per Servings 0.7g Carbs, 5g Protein, 3g Fat, 115 Calories

Tuna Topped Pickles

Servings: 5
Cooking Time: 0 Minutes
Ingredients:

- 1 tbsp fresh dill, and more for garnish
- ¼ cup full-fat mayonnaise
- 1 can light flaked tuna, drained
- 5 dill pickles
- ¼ tsp pepper

Directions:

1. Slice pickles in half, lengthwise. With a spoon, deseed the pickles and discard seeds.
2. In a small bowl, mix well the mayo, dill, and tuna using a fork.
3. Evenly divide them into 10 and spread over deseeded pickles.
4. Garnish with more dill on top and sprinkle black pepper.
5. Evenly divide into suggested servings and enjoy.

Nutrition Info:

- Info Per Servings 4g Carbs, 11g Protein, 14g Fat, 180 Calories

Parsnip And Carrot Fries With Aioli

Servings: 4

Cooking Time: 40 Minutes

Ingredients:

- 4 tbsp mayonnaise
- 2 garlic cloves, minced
- Salt and black pepper to taste
- 3 tbsp lemon juice
- Parsnip and Carrots Fries:
- 6 medium parsnips, julienned
- 3 large carrots, julienned
- 2 tbsp olive oil
- 5 tbsp chopped parsley
- Salt and black pepper to taste

Directions:

1. Preheat the oven to 400ºF. Make the aioli by mixing the mayonnaise with garlic, salt, pepper, and lemon juice; then refrigerate for 30 minutes.
2. Spread the parsnip and carrots on a baking sheet. Drizzle with olive oil, sprinkle with salt, and pepper, and rub the seasoning into the veggies. Bake for 35 minutes. Remove and transfer to a plate. Garnish the vegetables with parsley and serve with the chilled aioli.

Nutrition Info:

- Info Per Servings 4.4g Carbs, 2.1g Protein, 4.1g Fat, 205 Calories

Basil Keto Crackers

Servings: 6

Cooking Time: 15 Minutes

Ingredients:

- 1 ¼ cups almond flour
- ½ teaspoon baking powder
- ¼ teaspoon dried basil powder
- A pinch of cayenne pepper powder
- 1 clove of garlic, minced
- What you'll need from the store cupboard:
- Salt and pepper to taste
- 3 tablespoons oil

Directions:

1. Preheat oven to 350oF and lightly grease a cookie sheet with cooking spray.
2. Mix everything in a mixing bowl to create a dough.
3. Transfer the dough on a clean and flat working surface and spread out until 2mm thick. Cut into squares.
4. Place gently in an even layer on the prepped cookie sheet. Cook for 10 minutes.
5. Cook in batches.
6. Serve and enjoy.

Nutrition Info:

- Info Per Servings 2.9g Carbs, 5.3g Protein, 19.3g Fat, 205 Calories

Garlic Flavored Kale Taters

Servings: 4

Cooking Time: 20 Minutes

Ingredients:

- 4 cups kale, rinsed and chopped
- 2 cups cauliflower florets, finely chopped
- 2 tbsp almond milk
- 1 clove of garlic, minced
- 3 tablespoons oil
- 1/8 teaspoon black pepper
- cooking spray

Directions:

1. Heat oil in a large skillet and sauté the garlic for 2 minutes. Add the kale until it wilts. Transfer to a large bowl.
2. Add the almond milk. Season with pepper to taste.
3. Evenly divide into 4 and form patties.
4. Lightly grease a baking pan with cooking spray. Place patties on pan. Place pan on the top rack of the oven and broil on low for 6 minutes. Turnover patties and cook for another 4 minutes.
5. Serve and enjoy.

Nutrition Info:

- Info Per Servings 5g Carbs, 2g Protein, 11g Fat, 117 Calories

Choco And Coconut Bars

Servings: 9

Cooking Time: 30 Minutes

Ingredients:

- 1 tbsp Stevia
- ¾ cup shredded coconut, unsweetened
- ½ cup ground nuts (almonds, pecans, or walnuts)
- ¼ cup unsweetened cocoa powder
- 4 tbsp coconut oil

Directions:

1. In a medium bowl, mix shredded coconut, nuts, and cocoa powder.
2. Add Stevia and coconut oil.
3. Mix batter thoroughly.
4. In a 9x9 square inch pan or dish, press the batter and for a 30-minutes place in the freezer.
5. Evenly divide into suggested servings and enjoy.

Nutrition Info:

- Info Per Servings 2.7g Carbs, 1.3g Protein, 9.3g Fat, 99.7 Calories

Cheesy Cheddar Cauliflower

Servings: 6

Cooking Time: 20 Minutes

Ingredients:

- ½ cup butter
- 2 cups half and half cream
- 4 cups cheddar cheese, grated
- 3 cups cauliflower florets
- ½ cup water
- Pepper and salt to taste

Directions:

1. In a heavy-bottomed pot on medium-high fire, melt butter.
2. Stir in cream and cheddar cheese. Add in water. Mix well and cook for 5 minutes.
3. Add cauliflower florets and cook for 6 minutes. Season with pepper.
4. Serve and enjoy.

Nutrition Info:

- Info Per Servings 9g Carbs, 21g Protein, 42g Fat, 500 Calories

Coconut And Chocolate Bars

Servings: 6
Cooking Time: 30 Minutes
Ingredients:

- 1 tbsp Stevia
- ¾ cup shredded coconut, unsweetened
- ½ cup ground nuts (almonds, pecans, or walnuts)
- ¼ cup unsweetened cocoa powder
- 4 tbsp coconut oil
- Done

Directions:

1. In a medium bowl, mix shredded coconut, nuts, and cocoa powder.
2. Add Stevia and coconut oil.
3. Mix batter thoroughly.
4. In a 9x9 square inch pan or dish, press the batter and for a 30-minutes place in the freezer.
5. Serve and enjoy.

Nutrition Info:

- Info Per Servings 2.3g Carbs, 1.6g Protein, 17.8g Fat, 200 Calories

Nutty Avocado Crostini With Nori

Servings: 4
Cooking Time: 12 Minutes
Ingredients:

- 8 slices low carb baguette
- 4 nori sheets
- 1 cup mashed avocado
- ⅓ tsp salt
- 1 tsp lemon juice
- 1 ½ tbsp coconut oil
- ⅓ cup chopped raw walnuts
- 1 tbsp chia seeds

Directions:

1. In a bowl, flake the nori sheets into the smallest possible pieces.
2. In another bowl, mix the avocado, salt, and lemon juice, and stir in half of the nori flakes. Set aside.
3. Place the baguette on a baking sheet and toast in a broiler on medium heat for 2 minutes, making sure not to burn. Remove the crostini after and brush with coconut oil on both sides.
4. Top each crostini with the avocado mixture and garnish with the chia seeds, chopped walnuts, Serve the snack immediately.

Nutrition Info:

- Info Per Servings 2.8g Carbs, 13.7g Protein, 12.2g Fat, 195 Calories

Coconut Ginger Macaroons

Servings: 6
Cooking Time: 20 Minutes
Ingredients:

- 2 fingers ginger root, peeled and pureed
- 6 egg whites
- 1 cup finely shredded coconut
- ¼ cup swerve
- A pinch of chili powder
- 1 cup water
- Angel hair chili to garnish

Directions:

1. Preheat the oven to 350ºF and line a baking sheet with parchment paper. Set aside.
2. Then, in a heatproof bowl, whisk the ginger, egg whites, shredded coconut, swerve, and chili powder.
3. Bring the water to boil in a pot over medium heat and place the heatproof bowl on the pot. Then, continue whisking the mixture until it is glossy, about 4 minutes. Do not let the bowl touch the water or be too hot so that the eggs don't cook.
4. Spoon the mixture into the piping bag after and pipe out 40 to 50 little mounds on the lined baking sheet. Bake the macaroons in the middle part of the oven for 15 minutes.
5. Once they are ready, transfer them to a wire rack, garnish them with the angel hair chili, and serve.

Nutrition Info:

- Info Per Servings 0.3g Carbs, 6.8g Protein, 3.5g Fat, 97 Calories

Crab Stuffed Mushrooms

Servings: 3

Cooking Time: 25 Minutes

Ingredients:

- 2 tbsp minced green onion
- 1 cup cooked crabmeat, chopped finely
- ¼ cup Monterey Jack cheese, shredded
- 1 tsp lemon juice
- ¼ lb, fresh button mushrooms
- Pepper and salt to taste
- 3 tablespoons olive oil

Directions:

1. Destem mushrooms, wash, and drain well.
2. Chop mushroom stems.
3. Preheat oven to 400oF and lightly grease a baking pan with cooking spray.
4. In a small bowl, whisk well green onion, crabmeat, lemon juice, dill, and chopped mushroom stems.
5. Evenly spread mushrooms on prepared pan with cap sides up. Evenly spoon crabmeat mixture on top of mushroom caps.
6. Pop in the oven and bake for 20 minutes.
7. Remove from oven and sprinkle cheese on top.
8. Return to oven and broil for 3 minutes.
9. Serve and enjoy.

Nutrition Info:

- Info Per Servings 10g Carbs, 7.9g Protein, 17.3g Fat, 286 Calories

Balsamic Brussels Sprouts With Prosciutto

Servings: 4

Cooking Time: 40 Minutes

Ingredients:

- 3 tbsp balsamic vinegar
- 1 tbsp erythritol
- ½ tbsp olive oil
- Salt and black pepper to taste
- 1 lb Brussels sprouts, halved
- 5 slices prosciutto, chopped

Directions:

1. Preheat oven to 400ºF and line a baking sheet with parchment paper. Mix balsamic vinegar, erythritol, olive oil, salt, and black pepper and combine with the brussels sprouts in a bowl.

2. Spread the mixture on the baking sheet and roast for 30 minutes until tender on the inside and crispy on the outside. Toss with prosciutto, share among 4 plates, and serve with chicken breasts.

Nutrition Info:

- Info Per Servings 0g Carbs, 8g Protein, 14g Fat, 166 Calories

Easy Baked Parmesan Chips

Servings: 10

Cooking Time: 10 Minutes

Ingredients:

- 1 cup grated Parmesan cheese, low fat
- 1 tablespoon olive oil

Directions:

1. Lightly grease a cookie sheet and preheat oven to 400°F.
2. Evenly sprinkle parmesan cheese on a cookie sheet into 10 circles. Place them about ½-inch apart.
3. Drizzle with oil
4. Bake until lightly browned and crisped.
5. Let it cool, evenly divide into suggested servings and enjoy.

Nutrition Info:

- Info Per Servings 1.4g Carbs, 2.8g Protein, 12.8g Fat, 142 Calories

Shrimp Fra Diavolo

Servings: 3

Cooking Time: 5 Minutes

Ingredients:

- 3 tablespoons butter
- 1 onion, diced
- 5 cloves of garlic, minced
- 1 teaspoon red pepper flakes
- ¼ pound shrimps, shelled
- 2 tablespoons olive oil
- Salt and pepper to taste

Directions:

1. Heat the butter and the olive oil in a skillet and sauté the onion and garlic until fragrant.
2. Stir in the red pepper flakes and shrimps. Season with salt and pepper to taste.
3. Stir for 3 minutes.
4. Serve and enjoy.

Nutrition Info:

- Info Per Servings 4.5g Carbs, 21.0g Protein, 32.1g Fat, 388 Calories

Simple Tender Crisp Cauli-bites

Servings: 3

Cooking Time: 10 Minutes

Ingredients:

- 2 cups cauliflower florets
- 2 clove garlic minced
- 4 tablespoons olive oil
- ¼ tsp salt
- ½ tsp pepper

Directions:

1. In a small bowl, mix well olive oil salt, pepper, and garlic.
2. Place cauliflower florets on a baking pan. Drizzle with seasoned oil and toss well to coat.
3. Evenly spread in a single layer and place a pan on the top rack of the oven.
4. Broil on low for 5 minutes. Turnover florets and return to the oven.
5. Continue cooking for another 5 minutes.
6. Serve and enjoy.

Nutrition Info:

- Info Per Servings 4.9g Carbs, 1.7g Protein, 18g Fat, 183 Calories

Keto-approved Trail Mix

Servings: 8

Cooking Time: 3 Minutes

Ingredients:

- ¼ cup salted pumpkin seeds
- ½ cup slivered almonds
- ¾ cup roasted pecan halves
- ¼ cup unsweetened cranberries
- ¾ cup toasted coconut flakes

Directions:

1. In a skillet, place almonds and pecans. Heat for 2-3 minutes and let it cool.
2. Once cooled, in a large resealable plastic bag, combine all ingredients.
3. Seal and shake vigorously to mix.
4. Serve and enjoy.

Nutrition Info:

- Info Per Servings 8.0g Carbs, 4.4g Protein, 14.4g Fat, 184 Calories

Cajun Spiced Pecans

Servings: 10

Cooking Time: 10 Minutes

Ingredients:

- 1-pound pecan halves
- ¼ cup butter
- 1 packet Cajun seasoning mix
- ¼ teaspoon ground cayenne pepper
- Salt and pepper to taste

Directions:

1. Place a nonstick saucepan on medium fire and melt butter.
2. Add pecans and remaining ingredients.
3. Sauté for 5 minutes.
4. Remove from fire and let it cool completely.
5. Serve and enjoy.

Nutrition Info:

- Info Per Servings 6.8g Carbs, 4.2g Protein, 37.3g Fat, 356.5 Calories

Garlicky Cheddar Biscuits

Servings: 4

Cooking Time: 20 Minutes

Ingredients:

- ⅓ cup almond flour
- 2 tsp garlic powder
- Salt to taste
- 1 tsp low carb baking powder
- 5 eggs
- ⅓ cup butter, melted
- 1 ¼ cup grated sharp cheddar cheese
- ⅓ cup Greek yogurt

Directions:

1. Preheat the oven to 350ºF. Mix the flour, garlic powder, salt, baking powder, and cheddar, in a bowl.
2. In a separate bowl, whisk the eggs, butter, and Greek yogurt, and then pour the resulting mixture into the dry ingredients. Stir well until a dough-like consistency has formed.
3. Fetch half soupspoons of the mixture onto a baking sheet with 2-inch intervals between each batter. Bake them in the oven for 12 minutes to be golden brown and remove them after. Serve.

Nutrition Info:

- Info Per Servings 1.4g Carbs, 5.4g Protein, 14.2g Fat, 153 Calories

Bacon-flavored Kale Chips

Servings: 6
Cooking Time: 25 Minutes

Ingredients:

- 2 tbsp butter
- ¼ cup bacon grease
- 1-lb kale, around 1 bunch
- 1 to 2 tsp salt

Directions:

1. Remove the rib from kale leaves and tear it into 2-inch pieces.
2. Clean the kale leaves thoroughly and dry them inside a salad spinner.
3. In a skillet, add the butter to the bacon grease and warm the two fats under low heat. Add salt and stir constantly.
4. Set aside and let it cool.
5. Put the dried kale in a Ziploc back and add the cool liquid bacon grease and butter mixture.
6. Seal the Ziploc back and gently shake the kale leaves with the butter mixture. The leaves should have this shiny consistency, which means that they are coated evenly with the fat.
7. Pour the kale leaves on a cookie sheet and sprinkle more salt if necessary.
8. Bake for 25 minutes inside a preheated 350oF oven or until the leaves start to turn brown as well as crispy.

Nutrition Info:

- Info Per Servings 6.6g Carbs, 3.3g Protein, 13.1g Fat, 148 Calories

Garlic And Basil Mashed Celeriac

Servings: 4
Cooking Time: 30 Minutes

Ingredients:

- 2 lb celeriac, chopped
- 4 cups water
- 2 oz cream cheese
- 2 tbsp butter
- ⅓ cup sour cream
- ½ tsp garlic powder
- 2 tsp dried basil
- Salt and black pepper to taste

Directions:

1. Bring the celeriac and water to boil over high heat on a stovetop for 5 minutes and then reduce the heat to low to simmer for 15 minutes. Drain the celeriac through a colander after.
2. Then, pour the celeriac in a large bowl, add the cream cheese, butter, sour cream, garlic powder, dried basil, salt, and pepper. Mix them with a hand mixer on medium speed until well combined. Serve with pan-grilled salmon.

Nutrition Info:

- Info Per Servings 6g Carbs, 2.4g Protein, 0.5g Fat, 94 Calories

Buttered Broccoli

Servings: 6
Cooking Time: 10 Minutes

Ingredients:

- 1 broccoli head, florets only
- Salt and black pepper to taste
- ¼ cup butter

Directions:

1. Place the broccoli in a pot filled with salted water and bring to a boil. Cook for about 3 minutes.
2. Melt the butter in a microwave. Drain the broccoli and transfer to a plate. Drizzle the butter over and season with some salt and pepper.

Nutrition Info:

- Info Per Servings 5.5g Carbs, 3.9g Protein, 7.8g Fat, 114 Calories

Baba Ganoush Eggplant Dip

Servings: 4

Cooking Time: 80 Minutes

Ingredients:

- 1 head of garlic, unpeeled
- 1 large eggplant, cut in half lengthwise
- 5 tablespoons olive oil
- Lemon juice to taste
- 2 minced garlic cloves
- What you'll need from the store cupboard:
- Pepper and salt to taste

Directions:

1. With the rack in the middle position, preheat oven to 350°F.
2. Line a baking sheet with parchment paper. Place the eggplant cut side down on the baking sheet.
3. Roast until the flesh is very tender and pulls away easily from the skin, about 1 hour depending on the eggplant's size. Let it cool.
4. Meanwhile, cut the tips off the garlic cloves. Place the cloves in a square of aluminum foil. Fold up the edges of the foil and crimp together to form a tightly sealed packet. Roast alongside the eggplant until tender, about 20 minutes. Let cool.
5. Mash the cloves by pressing with a fork.
6. With a spoon, scoop the flesh from the eggplant and place it in the bowl of a food processor. Add the mashed garlic, oil and lemon juice. Process until smooth. Season with pepper.

Nutrition Info:

- Info Per Servings 10.2g Carbs, 1.6g Protein, 17.8g Fat, 192 Calories

Stuffed Jalapeno

Servings: 4

Cooking Time: 20 Minutes

Ingredients:

- 12 jalapeno peppers, halved lengthwise and seeded
- 2-oz cream cheese softened
- 2-oz shredded cheddar cheese
- ¼ cup almond meal
- Salt and pepper to taste

Directions:

1. Spray a cookie sheet with cooking spray and preheat oven to 400oF.
2. Equally fill each jalapeno with cheddar cheese, cream cheese, and sprinkle almond meal on top. Place on a prepped baking sheet.
3. Pop in oven and bake for 20 minutes.
4. Serve and enjoy.

Nutrition Info:

- Info Per Servings 7.7g Carbs, 5.9g Protein, 13.2g Fat, 187 Calories

Poultry Recipes

Stewed Italian Chicken

Servings: 4
Cooking Time: 25 Minutes
Ingredients:

- 3 ounces Italian dressing
- 4 boneless skinless chicken breasts thawed
- 5 tablespoons olive oil
- ½ cup water
- Salt and pepper to taste

Directions:

1. Add all ingredients in a pot on high fire and bring it to a boil.
2. Once boiling, lower fire to a simmer and cook for 20 minutes.
3. Adjust seasoning to taste.
4. Serve and enjoy.

Nutrition Info:

- Info Per Servings 3.6g Carbs, 53.6g Protein, 31.0g Fat, 545 Calories

Yummy Chicken Nuggets

Servings: 2
Cooking Time: 25 Minutes
Ingredients:

- ½ cup almond flour
- 1 egg
- 2 tbsp garlic powder
- 2 chicken breasts, cubed
- Salt and black pepper, to taste
- ½ cup butter

Directions:

1. Using a bowl, combine salt, garlic powder, flour, and pepper, and stir. In a separate bowl, beat the egg. Add the chicken breast cubes in egg mixture, then in the flour mixture. Set a pan over medium-high heat and warm butter, add in the chicken nuggets, and cook for 6 minutes on each side. Remove to paper towels, drain the excess grease and serve.

Nutrition Info:

- Info Per Servings 4.3g Carbs, 35g Protein, 37g Fat, 417 Calories

Habanero Chicken Wings

Servings: 4
Cooking Time: 65 Minutes
Ingredients:

- 2 pounds chicken wings
- Salt and black pepper, to taste
- 3 tbsp coconut aminos
- 2 tsp white vinegar
- 3 tbsp rice vinegar
- 3 tbsp stevia
- ¼ cup chives, chopped
- ½ tsp xanthan gum
- 5 dried habanero peppers, chopped

Directions:

1. Spread the chicken wings on a lined baking sheet, sprinkle with pepper and salt, set in an oven at 370ºF, and bake for 45 minutes. Put a small pan over medium heat, add in the white vinegar, coconut aminos, chives, stevia, rice vinegar, xanthan gum, and habanero peppers, bring the mixture to a boil, cook for 2 minutes, and remove from heat.
2. Dip the chicken wings into this sauce, lay them all on the baking sheet again, and bake for 10 more minutes. Serve warm.

Nutrition Info:

- Info Per Servings 2g Carbs, 26g Protein, 25g Fat, 416 Calories

Chicken, Eggplant And Gruyere Gratin

Servings: 4
Cooking Time: 55 Minutes
Ingredients:

- 3 tbsp butter
- 1 eggplant, chopped
- 2 tbsp gruyere cheese, grated
- Salt and black pepper, to taste
- 2 garlic cloves, minced
- 6 chicken thighs

Directions:

1. Set a pan over medium heat and warm 1 tablespoon butter, place in the chicken thighs, season with pepper and salt, cook each side for 3 minutes and lay them in a baking dish. In the same pan melt the rest of the butter and cook the garlic for 1 minute.

2. Stir in the eggplant, pepper, and salt, and cook for 10 minutes. Ladle this mixture over the chicken, spread with the cheese, set in the oven at 350ºF, and bake for 30 minutes. Turn on the oven's broiler, and broil everything for 2 minutes. Split among serving plates and enjoy.

Nutrition Info:

- Info Per Servings 5g Carbs, 34g Protein, 37g Fat, 412 Calories

Bacon And Chicken Cottage Pie

Servings: 4
Cooking Time: 55 Minutes
Ingredients:

- ½ cup onion, chopped
- 4 bacon slices
- 3 tbsp butter
- 1 carrot, chopped
- 3 garlic cloves, minced
- Salt and ground black pepper, to taste
- ¾ cup crème fraîche
- ½ cup chicken stock
- 12 ounces chicken breasts, cubed
- 2 tbsp Dijon mustard
- ¾ cup cheddar cheese, shredded
- For the dough
- ¾ cup almond flour
- 3 tbsp cream cheese
- 1½ cup mozzarella cheese, shredded
- 1 egg
- 1 tsp onion powder
- 1 tsp garlic powder
- 1 tsp Italian seasoning
- Salt and ground black pepper, to taste

Directions:

1. Set a pan over medium heat and warm butter and sauté the onion, garlic, pepper, bacon, salt, and carrot, for 5 minutes. Add in the chicken, and cook for 3 minutes. Stir in the crème fraîche, salt, mustard, pepper, and stock, cook for 7 minutes. Add in the cheddar and set aside.

2. Using a bowl, combine the mozzarella cheese with the cream cheese, and heat in a microwave for 1 minute. Stir in the garlic powder, salt, flour, pepper, Italian seasoning, onion powder, and egg. Knead the dough well, split into 4 pieces, and flatten each into a circle. Set the chicken mixture into 4 ramekins, top each with a dough circle, place in an oven at 370º F for 25 minutes.

Nutrition Info:

- Info Per Servings 8.2g Carbs, 41g Protein, 45g Fat, 571 Calories

Turkey Fajitas

Servings: 4

Cooking Time: 25 Minutes

Ingredients:

- 2 lb turkey breasts, skinless, boneless, sliced
- 1 tsp garlic powder
- 1 tsp chili powder
- 2 tsp cumin
- 2 tbsp lime juice
- Salt and black pepper, to taste
- 1 tsp sweet paprika
- 2 tbsp coconut oil
- 1 tsp ground coriander
- 1 green bell pepper, seeded, sliced
- 1 red bell pepper, seeded, sliced
- 1 onion, sliced
- 1 tbsp fresh cilantro, chopped
- 1 avocado, sliced
- 2 limes, cut into wedges

Directions:

1. Using a bowl, combine lime juice, cumin, garlic powder, coriander, paprika, salt, chili powder, and pepper. Toss in the turkey pieces to coat well. Set a pan over medium-high heat and warm oil, place in the turkey, cook each side for 3 minutes and set to a plate.

2. Add the remaining oil to the pan and warm over medium-high heat, stir in the bell peppers and onion, and cook for 6 minutes. Take the turkey back to the pan, add more seasonings if needed. Add a topping of fresh cilantro, lime wedges, and avocado and enjoy.

Nutrition Info:

- Info Per Servings 5g Carbs, 45g Protein, 32g Fat, 448 Calories

Spanish Chicken

Servings: 4

Cooking Time: 60 Minutes

Ingredients:

- 1/2 cup mushrooms, chopped
- 1 pound chorizo sausages, chopped
- 2 tbsp avocado oil
- 4 cherry peppers, chopped
- 1 red bell pepper, seeded, chopped
- 1 onion, peeled and sliced
- 2 tbsp garlic, minced
- 2 cups tomatoes, chopped
- 4 chicken thighs
- Salt and black pepper, to taste
- ½ cup chicken stock
- 1 tsp turmeric
- 1 tbsp vinegar
- 2 tsp dried oregano
- Fresh parsley, chopped, for serving

Directions:

1. Set a pan over medium heat and warm half of the avocado oil, stir in the chorizo sausages, and cook for 5-6 minutes until browned; remove to a bowl. Heat the rest of the oil, place in the chicken thighs, and apply pepper and salt for seasoning. Cook each side for 3 minutes and set aside on a bowl.

2. In the same pan, add the onion, bell pepper, cherry peppers, and mushrooms, and cook for 4 minutes. Stir in the garlic and cook for 2 minutes. Pour in the stock, turmeric, salt, tomatoes, pepper, vinegar, and oregano. Stir in the chorizo sausages and chicken, place everything to the oven at 400ºF, and bake for 30 minutes. Ladle into serving bowls and garnish with chopped parsley to serve.

Nutrition Info:

- Info Per Servings 4g Carbs, 25g Protein, 33g Fat, 415 Calories

Baked Chicken With Acorn Squash And Goat's Cheese

Servings: 6

Cooking Time: 1 Hour 15 Minutes

Ingredients:

- 6 chicken breasts, skinless and boneless
- 1 lb acorn squash, peeled and sliced
- Salt and ground black pepper, to taste
- 1 cup goat's cheese, shredded
- Cooking spray

Directions:

1. Take cooking oil and spray on a baking dish, add in chicken breasts, pepper, squash, and salt and drizzle with olive. Transfer in the oven set at 420ºF, and bake for 1 hour. Scatter goat's cheese, and bake for 15 minutes. Remove to a serving plate and enjoy.

Nutrition Info:

- Info Per Servings 5g Carbs, 12g Protein, 16g Fat, 235 Calories

Parmesan Wings With Yogurt Sauce

Servings: 6

Cooking Time: 25 Minutes

Ingredients:

- For the Dipping Sauce
- 1 cup plain yogurt
- 1 tsp fresh lemon juice
- Salt and black pepper to taste
- For the Wings
- 2 lb chicken wings
- Salt and black pepper to taste
- Cooking spray
- ½ cup melted butter
- ½ cup Hot sauce
- ¼ cup grated Parmesan cheese

Directions:

1. Mix the yogurt, lemon juice, salt, and black pepper in a bowl. Chill while making the chicken.

2. Preheat oven to 400ºF and season wings with salt and black pepper. Line them on a baking sheet and grease lightly with cooking spray. Bake for 20 minutes until golden brown. Mix butter, hot sauce, and parmesan in a bowl. Toss chicken in the sauce to evenly coat and plate. Serve with yogurt dipping sauce and celery strips.

Nutrition Info:

- Info Per Servings 4g Carbs, 24g Protein, 36.4g Fat, 452 Calories

Chicken Breasts With Walnut Crust

Servings: 4

Cooking Time: 30 Minutes

Ingredients:

- 1 egg, whisked
- Salt and black pepper, to taste
- 3 tbsp coconut oil
- 1½ cups walnuts, ground
- 4 chicken breast halves, boneless and skinless

Directions:

1. Using a bowl, add in walnuts and the whisked egg in another. Season the chicken, dip in the egg and then in pecans. Warm oil in a pan over medium-high heat and brown the chicken.

2. Remove the chicken pieces to a baking sheet, set in the oven, and bake for 10 minutes at 350º F. Serve topped with lemon slices.

Nutrition Info:

- Info Per Servings 1.5g Carbs, 35g Protein, 18g Fat, 322 Calories

Chicken Goujons With Tomato Sauce

Servings: 8

Cooking Time: 50 Minutes

Ingredients:

- 1½ pounds chicken breasts, skinless, boneless, cubed
- Salt and ground black pepper, to taste
- 1 egg
- 1 cup almond flour
- ¼ cup Parmesan cheese, grated
- ½ tsp garlic powder
- 1½ tsp dried parsley
- ½ tsp dried basil
- 4 tbsp avocado oil
- 4 cups spaghetti squash, cooked
- 6 oz gruyere cheese, shredded
- 1½ cups tomato sauce
- Fresh basil, chopped, for serving

Directions:

1. Using a bowl, combine the almond flour with 1 teaspoon parsley, Parmesan cheese, pepper, garlic powder, and salt. In a separate bowl, combine the egg with pepper and salt. Dip the chicken in the egg, and then in almond flour mixture.
2. Set a pan over medium-high heat and warm 3 tablespoons avocado oil, add in the chicken, cook until golden, and remove to paper towels. Using a bowl, combine the spaghetti squash with salt, dried basil, rest of the parsley, 1 tablespoon avocado oil, and pepper.
3. Sprinkle this into a baking dish, top with the chicken pieces, followed by the marinara sauce. Scatter shredded gruyere cheese on top, and bake for 30 minutes at 360ºF. Remove, and sprinkle with fresh basil before serving.

Nutrition Info:

- Info Per Servings 5g Carbs, 28g Protein, 36g Fat, 415 Calories

Pesto Chicken

Servings: 4

Cooking Time: 30 Minutes

Ingredients:

- 2 cups basil leaves
- ¼ cup + 1 tbsp extra virgin olive oil, divided
- 5 sun-dried tomatoes
- 4 chicken breasts
- 6 cloves garlic, smashed, peeled, and minced
- What you'll need from the store cupboard:
- Salt and pepper to taste
- Water

Directions:

1. Put in the food processor the basil leaves, ¼ cup olive oil, and tomatoes. Season with salt and pepper to taste. Add a cup of water if needed.
2. Season chicken breasts with pepper and salt generously.
3. On medium fire, heat a saucepan for 2 minutes. Add a tbsp of olive oil to the pan and swirl to coat bottom and sides. Heat oil for a minute.
4. Add chicken and sear for 5 minutes per side.
5. Add pesto sauce, cover, and cook on low fire for 15 minutes or until chicken is cooked thoroughly.
6. Serve and enjoy.

Nutrition Info:

- Info Per Servings 1.1g Carbs, 60.8g Protein, 32.7g Fat, 556 Calories

Herby Chicken Meatballs

Servings: 3

Cooking Time: 25 Minutes

Ingredients:

- 1 pound ground chicken
- Salt and black pepper, to taste
- 2 tbsp ranch dressing
- ½ cup almond flour
- ¼ cup mozzarella cheese, grated
- 1 tbsp dry Italian seasoning
- ¼ cup hot sauce + more for serving
- 1 egg

Directions:

1. Using a bowl, combine chicken meat, pepper, ranch dressing, Italian seasoning, flour, hot sauce, mozzarella cheese, salt, and the egg. Form 9 meatballs, arrange them on a lined baking tray and cook for 16 minutes at 480°F. Place the chicken meatballs in a bowl and serve along with hot sauce.

Nutrition Info:

- Info Per Servings 2.1g Carbs, 32g Protein, 31g Fat, 456 Calories

Chicken, Broccoli & Cashew Stir-fry

Servings: 4

Cooking Time: 30 Minutes

Ingredients:

- 2 chicken breasts, cut into strips
- 3 tbsp olive oil
- 2 tbsp soy sauce
- 2 tsp white wine vinegar
- 1 tsp erythritol
- 2 tsp xanthan gum
- 1 lemon, juiced
- 1 cup unsalted cashew nuts
- 2 cups broccoli florets
- 1 white onion, thinly sliced
- Pepper to taste

Directions:

1. In a bowl, mix the soy sauce, vinegar, lemon juice, erythritol, and xanthan gum. Set aside.
2. Heat the oil in a wok and fry the cashew for 4 minutes until golden-brown. Remove the cashews into a paper towel lined plate and set aside. Sauté the onion in the same oil for 4 minutes until soft and browned; add to the cashew nuts.
3. Add the chicken to the wok and cook for 4 minutes; include the broccoli and pepper. Stir-fry and pour the soy sauce mixture in. Stir and cook the sauce for 4 minutes and pour in the cashews and onion. Stir once more, cook for 1 minute, and turn the heat off.
4. Serve the chicken stir-fry with some steamed cauli rice.

Nutrition Info:

- Info Per Servings 3.4g Carbs, 17.3g Protein, 10.1g Fat, 286 Calories

Spinach Artichoke Heart Chicken

Servings: 4
Cooking Time: 30 Minutes
Ingredients:

- 4 chicken breasts
- 1 package frozen spinach
- 1 package cream cheese, softened
- ½ can quartered artichoke hearts, drained and chopped
- ¼ cup. shredded Parmesan cheese
- ¼ cup. mayonnaise
- 2 tbsp. olive oil
- 2 tbsps. grated mozzarella cheese
- ½ teaspoon. garlic powder
- Salt to taste

Directions:

1. Place the spinach in a bowl and microwave for 2 to 3 minutes. Let chill and drain.
2. Stir in cream cheese, artichoke hearts, Parmesan cheese, mayonnaise, garlic powder, and salt, whisk together. Cut chicken breasts to an even thickness. Spread salt and pepper over chicken breasts per side.
3. Preheat oven to 375 degrees F.
4. In a large skillet over medium-high, heat olive oil for 2 to 3 minutes. Lay chicken breasts in a large baking dish, pour spinach-artichoke mixture over chicken breasts. Place in the oven and bake at least 165 degrees F.
5. Sprinkle with mozzarella cheese and bake for 1 to 2 minutes more. Serve and enjoy.

Nutrition Info:

- Info Per Servings 5.4g Carbs, 56g Protein, 33.3g Fat, 554 Calories

Chicken Skewers With Celery Fries

Servings: 4
Cooking Time: 60 Minutes
Ingredients:

- 2 chicken breasts
- ½ tsp salt
- ¼ tsp ground black pepper
- 2 tbsp olive oil
- 1/4 chicken broth
- For the fries
- 1 lb celery root
- 2 tbsp olive oil
- ½ tsp salt
- ¼ tsp ground black pepper

Directions:

1. Set an oven to 400ºF. Grease and line a baking sheet. In a large bowl, mix oil, spices and the chicken; set in the fridge for 10 minutes while covered. Peel and chop celery root to form fry shapes and place into a separate bowl. Apply oil to coat and add pepper and salt for seasoning. Arrange to the baking tray in an even layer and bake for 10 minutes.
2. Take the chicken from the refrigerator and thread onto the skewers. Place over the celery, pour in the chicken broth, then set in the oven for 30 minutes. Serve with lemon wedges.

Nutrition Info:

- Info Per Servings 6g Carbs, 39g Protein, 43g Fat, 579 Calories

Zucchini Spaghetti With Turkey Bolognese Sauce

Servings: 6
Cooking Time: 30 Minutes
Ingredients:

- 2 cups sliced mushrooms
- 2 tsp olive oil
- 1 pound ground turkey
- 3 tbsp pesto sauce
- 1 cup diced onion
- 2 cups broccoli florets
- 6 cups zucchini, spiralized

Directions:

1. Heat the oil in a skillet. Add zucchini and cook for 2-3 minutes, stirring continuously; set aside.
2. Add turkey to the skillet and cook until browned, about 7-8 minutes. Transfer to a plate. Add onion and cook until translucent, about 3 minutes. Add broccoli and mushrooms, and cook for 7 more minutes. Return the turkey to the skillet. Stir in the pesto sauce. Cover the pan, lower the heat, and simmer for 15 minutes. Stir in zucchini pasta and serve immediately.

Nutrition Info:

- Info Per Servings 3.8g Carbs, 19g Protein, 16g Fat, 273 Calories

Chicken And Green Cabbage Casserole

Servings: 4
Cooking Time: 55 Minutes
Ingredients:

- 3 cups cheddar cheese, grated
- 10 ounces green cabbage, shredded
- 3 chicken breasts, skinless, boneless, cooked, cubed
- 1 cup mayonnaise
- 1 tbsp coconut oil, melted
- ⅓ cup chicken stock
- Salt and ground black pepper, to taste
- Juice of 1 lemon

Directions:

1. Apply oil to a baking dish, and set chicken pieces to the bottom. Spread green cabbage, followed by half of the cheese. Using a bowl, combine the mayonnaise with pepper, stock, lemon juice, and salt.
2. Pour this mixture over the chicken, spread the rest of the cheese, cover with aluminum foil, and bake for 30 minutes in the oven at 350ºF. Open the aluminum foil, and cook for 20 more minutes.

Nutrition Info:

- Info Per Servings 6g Carbs, 25g Protein, 15g Fat, 231 Calories

Stuffed Avocados With Chicken

Servings: 2
Cooking Time: 10 Minutes
Ingredients:

- 2 avocados, cut in half and pitted
- ¼ cup pesto
- 1 tsp dried thyme
- 2 tbsp cream cheese
- 1½ cups chicken, cooked and shredded
- Salt and ground black pepper, to taste
- ¼ tsp cayenne pepper
- ½ tsp onion powder
- ½ tsp garlic powder
- 1 tsp paprika
- Salt and black pepper, to taste
- 2 tbsp lemon juice

Directions:

1. Scoop the insides of the avocado halves, and place the flesh in a bowl. Add in the chicken. Stir in the remaining ingredients. Stuff the avocado cups with chicken mixture and enjoy.

Nutrition Info:

- Info Per Servings 5g Carbs, 24g Protein, 40g Fat, 511 Calories

Stewed Chicken Salsa

Servings: 4
Cooking Time: 25 Minutes
Ingredients:

- 1 cup shredded cheddar cheese
- 8-ounces cream cheese
- 16-ounces salsa
- 4 skinless and boneless thawed chicken breasts
- 4 tablespoons butter
- 1 cup water

Directions:

1. Add all ingredients in a pot, except for sour cream, on high fire, and bring to a boil.
2. Once boiling, lower fire to a simmer and cook for 20 minutes.
3. Adjust seasoning to taste and stir in sour cream.
4. Serve and enjoy.

Nutrition Info:

- Info Per Servings 9.6g Carbs, 67.8g Protein, 32.6g Fat, 658 Calories

One-pot Chicken With Mushrooms And Spinach

Servings: 4

Cooking Time: 40 Minutes

Ingredients:

- 4 chicken thighs
- 2 cups mushrooms, sliced
- 1 cup spinach, chopped
- ¼ cup butter
- Salt and black pepper, to taste
- ½ tsp onion powder
- ½ tsp garlic powder
- ½ cup water
- 1 tsp Dijon mustard
- 1 tbsp fresh tarragon, chopped

Directions:

1. Set a pan over medium-high heat and warm half of the butter, place in the thighs, and sprinkle with onion powder, pepper, garlic powder, and salt. Cook each side for 3 minutes and set on a plate.

2. Place the remaining butter to the same pan and warm. Stir in mushrooms and cook for 5 minutes. Place in water and mustard, take the chicken pieces back to the pan, and cook for 15 minutes while covered. Stir in the tarragon and spinach, and cook for 5 minutes.

Nutrition Info:

- Info Per Servings 1g Carbs, 32g Protein, 23g Fat, 453 Calories

Chicken Breasts With Cheddar & Pepperoni

Servings: 4

Cooking Time: 40 Minutes

Ingredients:

- 12 oz canned tomato sauce
- 1 tbsp olive oil
- 4 chicken breast halves, skinless and boneless
- Salt and ground black pepper, to taste
- 1 tsp dried oregano
- 4 oz cheddar cheese, sliced
- 1 tsp garlic powder
- 2 oz pepperoni, sliced

Directions:

1. Preheat your oven to 390°F. Using a bowl, combine chicken with oregano, salt, garlic, and pepper.

2. Heat a pan with the olive oil over medium-high heat, add in the chicken, cook each side for 2 minutes, and remove to a baking dish. Top with the cheddar cheese slices spread the sauce, then cover with pepperoni slices. Bake for 30 minutes. Serve warm garnished with fresh oregano if desired

Nutrition Info:

- Info Per Servings 4.5g Carbs, 32g Protein, 21g Fat, 387 Calories

Cheesy Chicken Bake With Zucchini

Servings: 12

Cooking Time: 45 Minutes

Ingredients:

- 2 lb chicken breasts, cubed
- 1 tbsp butter
- 1 cup green bell peppers, sliced
- 1 cup yellow onions, sliced
- 1 zucchini, sliced
- 2 garlic cloves, divided
- 2 tsp Italian seasoning
- ½ tsp salt
- ½ tsp black pepper
- 8 oz cream cheese, softened
- ½ cup mayonnaise
- 2 tbsp Worcestershire sauce (sugar-free)
- 2 cups cheddar cheese, shredded

Directions:

1. Set oven to 370ºF and grease and line a baking dish.
2. Set a pan over medium-high heat. Place in the butter and let melt, then add in the chicken.
3. Cook until browned. Place in onions, zucchini, black pepper, garlic, peppers, salt, and 1 tsp of Italian seasonings. Cook unti tender. Set aside.
4. In a bowl, mix cream cheese, garlic, cheddar cheese, remaining seasoning, mayonnaise, and Worcestershire sauce. Stir in mea Place the mixture into the prepared baking dish then set into the oven. Cook until browned for 30 minutes.

Nutrition Info:

- Info Per Servings 4.5g Carbs, 21g Protein, 37g Fat, 489 Calories

Bacon Chicken Alfredo

Servings: 4

Cooking Time: 35 Minutes

Ingredients:

- 4-ounces mushrooms drained and sliced
- 1 cup shredded mozzarella cheese
- 1 jar Classico creamy alfredo sauce
- 6 slices chopped hickory bacon
- 4 boneless skinless chicken breasts thawed or fresh
- Pepper and salt to taste
- ½ cup water

Directions:

1. Add all ingredients in a pot on high fire and bring it to a boil.
2. Once boiling, lower fire to a simmer and cook for 30 minutes, stirring every now and then.
3. Adjust seasoning to taste.
4. Serve and enjoy.

Nutrition Info:

- Info Per Servings 7.7g Carbs, 75.8g Protein, 70.8g Fat, 976 Calories

Thyme Chicken Thighs

Servings: 4

Cooking Time: 30 Minutes

Ingredients:

- ½ cup chicken stock
- 1 tbsp olive oil
- ½ cup chopped onion
- 4 chicken thighs
- ¼ cup heavy cream
- 2 tbsp Dijon mustard
- 1 tsp thyme
- 1 tsp garlic powder

Directions:

1. Heat the olive oil in a pan. Cook the chicken for about 4 minutes per side. Set aside. Sauté the onion in the same pan for 3 minutes, add the stock, and simmer for 5 minutes. Stir in mustard and heavy cream, along with thyme and garlic powder. Pour the sauce over the chicken and serve.

Nutrition Info:

- Info Per Servings 4g Carbs, 33g Protein, 42g Fat, 528 Calories

Garlic & Ginger Chicken With Peanut Sauce

Servings: 6

Cooking Time: 1 Hour And 50 Minutes

Ingredients:

- 1 tbsp wheat-free soy sauce
- 1 tbsp sugar-free fish sauce
- 1 tbsp lime juice
- 1 tsp cilantro
- 1 tsp minced garlic
- 1 tsp minced ginger
- 1 tbsp olive oil
- 1 tbsp rice wine vinegar
- 1 tsp cayenne pepper
- 1 tsp erythritol
- 6 chicken thighs
- Sauce:
- ½ cup peanut butter
- 1 tsp minced garlic
- 1 tbsp lime juice
- 2 tbsp water
- 1 tsp minced ginger
- 1 tbsp chopped jalapeño
- 2 tbsp rice wine vinegar
- 2 tbsp erythritol
- 1 tbsp fish sauce

Directions:

1. Combine all chicken ingredients in a large Ziploc bag. Seal the bag and shake to combine. Refrigerate for 1 hour. Remove from fridge about 15 minutes before cooking.

2. Preheat the grill to medium and grill the chicken for 7 minutes per side. Whisk together all sauce ingredients in a mixing bowl. Serve the chicken drizzled with peanut sauce.

Nutrition Info:

- Info Per Servings 3g Carbs, 35g Protein, 36g Fat, 492 Calories

Pork, Beef & Lamb Recipes

Pork Chops With Cranberry Sauce

Servings: 6

Cooking Time: 30 Minutes

Ingredients:

- 6-pieces bone-in pork loin chops
- 1 14-ounce fresh cranberries, pitted
- 5 tablespoons butter
- Salt and pepper to taste
- 1 cup water

Directions:

1. Add all ingredients in a pot on high fire and bring to a boil.
2. Once boiling, lower fire to a simmer and cook for 25 minutes.
3. Adjust seasoning to taste.
4. Serve and enjoy.

Nutrition Info:

- Info Per Servings 9.7g Carbs, 40.6g Protein, 27.6g Fat, 452 Calories

Pork Burgers With Caramelized Onion Rings

Servings: 6

Cooking Time: 20 Minutes

Ingredients:

- 2 lb ground pork
- Pink salt and chili pepper to taste
- 3 tbsp olive oil
- 1 tbsp butter
- 1 white onion, sliced into rings
- 1 tbsp balsamic vinegar
- 3 drops liquid stevia
- 6 low carb burger buns, halved
- 2 firm tomatoes, sliced into rings

Directions:

1. Combine the pork, salt and chili pepper in a bowl and mold out 6 patties.
2. Heat the olive oil in a skillet over medium heat and fry the patties for 4 to 5 minutes on each side until golden brown on the outside. Remove onto a plate and sit for 3 minutes.
3. Meanwhile, melt butter in a skillet over medium heat, sauté the onions for 2 minutes to be soft, and stir in the balsamic vinegar and liquid stevia.
4. Cook for 30 seconds stirring once or twice until caramelized. In each bun, place a patty, top with some onion rings and 2 tomato rings. Serve the burgers with cheddar cheese dip.

Nutrition Info:

- Info Per Servings 7.6g Carbs, 26g Protein, 32g Fat, 445 Calories

Creamy Pork Chops

Servings: 3
Cooking Time: 50 Minutes
Ingredients:

- 8 ounces mushrooms, sliced
- 1 tsp garlic powder
- 1 onion, peeled and chopped
- 1 cup heavy cream
- 3 pork chops, boneless
- 1 tsp ground nutmeg
- ¼ cup coconut oil

Directions:

1. Set a pan over medium heat and warm the oil, add in the onions and mushrooms, and cook for 4 minutes. Stir in the pork chops, season with garlic powder, and nutmeg, and sear until browned.
2. Put the pan in the oven at 350ºF, and bake for 30 minutes. Remove pork chops to bowls and maintain warm. Place the pan over medium heat, pour in the heavy cream and vinegar over the mushrooms mixture, and cook for 5 minutes; remove from heat. Sprinkle sauce over pork chops and enjoy.

Nutrition Info:

- Info Per Servings 6.8g Carbs, 42g Protein, 40g Fat, 612 Calories

Russian Beef Gratin

Servings: 5
Cooking Time: 45 Minutes
Ingredients:

- 2 tsp onion flakes
- 2 pounds ground beef
- 2 garlic cloves, minced
- Salt and ground black pepper, to taste
- 1 cup mozzarella cheese, shredded
- 2 cups fontina cheese, shredded
- 1 cup Russian dressing
- 2 tbsp sesame seeds, toasted
- 20 dill pickle slices
- 1 iceberg lettuce head, torn

Directions:

1. Set a pan over medium heat, place in the beef, garlic, salt, onion flakes, and pepper, and cook for 5 minutes. Remove and set to a baking dish, stir in half of the Russian dressing, mozzarella cheese, and spread 1 cup of the fontina cheese.
2. Lay the pickle slices on top, spread over the remaining fontina cheese and sesame seeds, place in the oven at 350ºF, and bake for 20 minutes. Split the lettuce on serving plates, apply a topping of beef gratin, and the remaining Russian dressing.

Nutrition Info:

- Info Per Servings 5g Carbs, 41g Protein, 48g Fat, 584 Calories

Grilled Lamb On Lemony Sauce

Servings: 4
Cooking Time: 25 Minutes
Ingredients:

- 8 lamb chops
- 2 tbsp favorite spice mix
- 1 tsp olive oil
- Sauce:
- ¼ cup olive oil
- 1 tsp red pepper flakes
- 2 tbsp lemon juice
- 2 tbsp fresh mint
- 3 garlic cloves, pressed
- 2 tbsp lemon zest
- ¼ cup parsley
- ½ tsp smoked paprika

Directions:

1. Rub the lamb with the oil and sprinkle with the seasoning. Preheat the grill to medium. Grill the lamb chops for about 3 minutes per side. Whisk together the sauce ingredients. Serve the lamb chops with the sauce.

Nutrition Info:

- Info Per Servings 1g Carbs, 29g Protein, 31g Fat, 392 Calories

Spiced Baked Pork With Milk

Servings: 4

Cooking Time: 2h 30 Minutes

Ingredients:

- 3 1/2 pounds boneless pork shoulder, cut into large pieces
- 1 tablespoon freshly ground black pepper
- 2 bay leaves
- 1/4 teaspoon cayenne pepper
- 2 cups almond milk
- 1 tablespoon kosher salt, or more to taste
- 2 tablespoons olive oil
- 1 lime, juiced
- 2 teaspoons ground cumin
- 1 teaspoon dried oregano

Directions:

1. Heat oil in a large pot over high heat. Cook pork with pepper and salt for 5 minutes.
2. Return all cooked pork and accumulated juice to pot. Season pork with bay leaves, cumin, dried oregano, and cayenne pepper.
3. Stir in fresh lime juice, orange zest, and milk. Bring mixture to a boil over high heat; reduce heat to low. Cover and simmer stirring occasionally, about 2 hours.
4. Preheat oven to 450 degrees F.
5. Skim the fat to grease a baking dish. Transfer the pieces of pork to the baking dish. Drizzle about 2 more tablespoons of olive oil over the meat.
6. Bake in preheated oven for about 15 minutes until cooked through.

Nutrition Info:

- Info Per Servings 3.7g Carbs, 22.4g Protein, 24.1g Fat, 325 Calories

Caribbean Beef

Servings: 8

Cooking Time: 1 Hour 10 Minutes

Ingredients:

- 2 onions, chopped
- 2 tbsp avocado oil
- 2 pounds beef stew meat, cubed
- 2 red bell peppers, seeded and chopped
- 1 habanero pepper, chopped
- 4 green chilies, chopped
- 14.5 ounces canned diced tomatoes
- 2 tbsp fresh cilantro, chopped
- 4 garlic cloves, minced
- ½ cup vegetable broth
- Salt and black pepper, to taste
- 1 ½ tsp cumin
- ½ cup black olives, chopped
- 1 tsp dried oregano

Directions:

1. Set a pan over medium-high heat and warm avocado oil. Brown the beef on all sides; remove and set aside. Stir-fry in the red bell peppers, green chilies, oregano, garlic, habanero pepper, onions, and cumin, for about 5-6 minutes. Pour in the tomatoes and broth, and cook for 1 hour. Stir in the olives, adjust the seasonings and serve in bowls sprinkled with fresh cilantro.

Nutrition Info:

- Info Per Servings 8g Carbs, 25g Protein, 14g Fat, 305 Calories

Pork Osso Bucco

Servings: 6

Cooking Time: 1 Hour 55 Minutes

Ingredients:

- 4 tbsp butter, softened
- 6 pork shanks
- 2 tbsp olive oil
- 3 cloves garlic, minced
- 1 cup diced tomatoes
- Salt and black pepper to taste
- ½ cup chopped onions
- ½ cup chopped celery
- ½ cup chopped carrots
- 2 cups Cabernet Sauvignon
- 5 cups beef broth
- ½ cup chopped parsley + extra to garnish
- 2 tsp lemon zest

Directions:

1. Melt the butter in a large saucepan over medium heat. Season the pork with salt and pepper and brown it for 12 minutes; remove to a plate.

2. In the same pan, sauté 2 cloves of garlic and onions in the oil, for 3 minutes then return the pork shanks. Stir in the Cabernet, carrots, celery, tomatoes, and beef broth with a season of salt and pepper. Cover the pan and let it simmer on low heat for 1 ½ hours basting the pork every 15 minutes with the sauce.

3. In a bowl, mix the remaining garlic, parsley, and lemon zest to make a gremolata, and stir the mixture into the sauce when it is ready. Turn the heat off and dish the Osso Bucco. Garnish with parsley and serve with a creamy turnip mash.

Nutrition Info:

- Info Per Servings 6.1g Carbs, 34g Protein, 40g Fat, 590 Calories

Homemade Classic Beef Burgers

Servings: 4

Cooking Time: 15 Minutes

Ingredients:

- 1 pound ground beef
- ½ tsp onion powder
- ½ tsp garlic powder
- 2 tbsp ghee
- 1 tsp Dijon mustard
- 4 low carb buns, halved
- ¼ cup mayonnaise
- 1 tsp sriracha
- 4 tbsp cabbage slaw

Directions:

1. Mix together the beef, onion, garlic powder, mustard, salt, and black pepper; create 4 burgers. Melt the ghee in a skillet and cook the burgers for about 3 minutes per side. Serve in buns topped with mayo, sriracha, and slaw.

Nutrition Info:

- Info Per Servings 7.9g Carbs, 39g Protein, 55g Fat, 664 Calories

Filling Beefy Soup

Servings: 4

Cooking Time: 15 Minutes

Ingredients:

- 1 small onion, diced
- 3 cloves of garlic, minced
- 1-pound lean ground sirloin
- 3 cups low-sodium beef broth
- 1 bag frozen vegetables of your choice
- 5 tablespoons oil
- Black pepper and salt to taste

Directions:

1. In a large saucepan, heat the oil over medium heat and sauté the onion and garlic until fragrant.
2. Stir in the lean ground sirloin and cook for 3 minutes until lightly golden.
3. Add in the rest of the ingredients and bring the broth to a boil for 10 minutes.
4. Serve warm.

Nutrition Info:

- Info Per Servings 5.0g Carbs, 29.0g Protein, 34.0g Fat, 334 Calories

Beef With Dilled Yogurt

Servings: 6

Cooking Time: 25 Minutes

Ingredients:

- ¼ cup almond milk
- 2 pounds ground beef
- 1 onion, grated
- 5 zero carb bread slices, torn
- 1 egg, whisked
- ¼ cup fresh parsley, chopped
- Salt and black pepper, to taste
- 2 garlic cloves, minced
- ¼ cup fresh mint, chopped
- 2 ½ tsp dried oregano
- ¼ cup olive oil
- 1 cup cherry tomatoes, halved
- 1 cucumber, sliced
- 1 cup baby spinach
- 1½ tbsp lemon juice
- 1 cup dilled Greek yogurt

Directions:

1. Place the torn bread in a bowl, add in the milk, and set aside for 3 minutes. Squeeze the bread, chop, and place into a bowl. Stir in the beef, salt, mint, onion, parsley, pepper, egg, oregano, and garlic.
2. Form balls out of this mixture and place on a working surface. Set a pan over medium heat and warm half of the oil; fry the meatballs for 8 minutes. Flip occasionally, and set aside in a tray.
3. In a salad plate, combine the spinach with the cherry tomatoes and cucumber. Mix in the remaining oil, lemon juice, black pepper, and salt. Spread dilled yogurt over, and top with meatballs to serve.

Nutrition Info:

- Info Per Servings 8.3g Carbs, 27g Protein, 22.4g Fat, 408 Calories

Beef Stuffed Roasted Squash

Servings: 4

Cooking Time: 1 Hour 15 Minutes

Ingredients:

- 2 lb butternut squash, pricked with a fork
- Salt and ground black pepper, to taste
- 3 garlic cloves, minced
- 1 onion, peeled and chopped
- 1 button mushroom, sliced
- 28 ounces canned diced tomatoes
- 1 tsp dried oregano
- ¼ tsp cayenne pepper
- ½ tsp dried thyme
- 1 pound ground beef
- 1 green bell pepper, chopped

Directions:

1. Lay the butternut squash on a lined baking sheet, set in the oven at 400ºF, and bake for 40 minutes. Cut in half, set aside to let cool, deseed, scoop out most of the flesh and let sit. Heat a greased pan over medium-high heat, add in the garlic, mushrooms, onion, and beef, and cook until the meat browns.
2. Stir in the green pepper, salt, thyme, tomatoes, oregano, black pepper, and cayenne, and cook for 10 minutes; stir in the flesh. Stuff the squash halves with the beef mixture, and bake in the oven for 10 minutes. Split into plates and enjoy.

Nutrition Info:

- Info Per Servings 12.4g Carbs, 34g Protein, 14.7g Fat, 406 Calories

Garlic Lime Marinated Pork Chops

Servings: 4

Cooking Time: 10 Minutes

Ingredients:

- 4 6-ounce lean boneless pork chops, trimmed from fat
- 4 cloves of garlic, crushed
- 1 teaspoon cumin
- 1 teaspoon paprika
- ½ lime, juiced and zested
- 1 tsp black pepper
- ½ tsp salt
- 5 tablespoons olive oil

Directions:

1. In a bowl, season the pork with the rest of the ingredients.
2. Allow marinating inside the fridge for at least 2 hours.
3. Place the pork chops in a baking dish or broiler pan and grill for 5 minutes on each side until golden brown.
4. Serve with salad if desired.

Nutrition Info:

- Info Per Servings 2.4g Carbs, 38.5g Protein, 22.9g Fat, 376 Calories

Simple Beef Curry

Servings: 6

Cooking Time:30 Minutes

Ingredients:

- 2 pounds boneless beef chuck
- 1 tbsp ground turmeric
- 1 tsp ginger paste
- 6 cloves garlic, minced
- 1 onion, chopped
- 3 tbsp olive oil
- 1 cup water
- Pepper and salt to taste

Directions:

1. In a saucepan, heat the olive oil over medium heat then add onion and garlic for 5 minutes.
2. Stir in beef and sauté for 10 minutes.
3. Add remaining ingredients, cover, and simmer for 20 minutes.
4. Adjust seasoning if needed.
5. Serve and enjoy.

Nutrition Info:

- Info Per Servings 5.0g Carbs, 33.0g Protein, 16.0g Fat, 287 Calories

Beef Stew With Bacon

Servings: 6

Cooking Time: 1 Hour 15 Minutes

Ingredients:

- 8 ounces bacon, chopped
- 4 lb beef meat for stew, cubed
- 4 garlic cloves, minced
- 2 brown onions, chopped
- 2 tbsp olive oil
- 4 tbsp red vinegar
- 4 cups beef stock
- 2 tbsp tomato puree
- 2 cinnamon sticks
- 3 lemon peel strips
- ½ cup fresh parsley, chopped
- 4 thyme sprigs
- 2 tbsp butter
- Salt and black pepper, to taste

Directions:

1. Set a saucepan over medium-high heat and warm oil, add in the garlic, bacon, and onion, and cook for 5 minutes. Stir in the beef, and cook until slightly brown. Pour in the vinegar, pepper, butter, lemon peel strips, stock, salt, tomato puree, cinnamon sticks and thyme; stir for 3 minutes.

2. Cook for 1 hour while covered. Get rid of the thyme, lemon peel, and cinnamon sticks. Split into serving bowls and sprinkle with parsley to serve.

Nutrition Info:

- Info Per Servings 5.7g Carbs, 63g Protein, 36g Fat, 592 Calories

Adobo Beef Fajitas

Servings: 4

Cooking Time: 35 Minutes

Ingredients:

- 2 lb skirt steak, cut in halves
- 2 tbsp Adobo seasoning
- Pink salt to taste
- 2 tbsp olive oil
- 2 large white onion, chopped
- 1 cup sliced mixed bell peppers, chopped
- 12 low carb tortillas

Directions:

1. Season the steak with adobo and marinate in the fridge for one hour.
2. Preheat grill to 425ºF and cook steak for 6 minutes on each side, flipping once until lightly browned. Remove from heat and wrap in foil and let sit for 10 minutes. This allows the meat to cook in its heat for a few more minutes before slicing.
3. Heat the olive oil in a skillet over medium heat and sauté the onion and bell peppers for 5 minutes or until soft. Cut steak against the grain into strips and share on the tortillas. Top with the veggies and serve with guacamole.

Nutrition Info:

- Info Per Servings 5g Carbs, 18g Protein, 25g Fat, 348 Calories

New York Strip Steak With Mushroom Sauce

Servings: 2

Cooking Time: 20 Minutes

Ingredients:

- 2 New York Strip steaks, trimmed from fat
- 3 cloves of garlic, minced
- 2 ounces shiitake mushrooms, sliced
- 2 ounces button mushrooms, sliced
- ¼ teaspoon thyme
- ¼ cup water
- ½ tsp salt
- 1 tsp pepper
- 5 tablespoons olive oil

Directions:

1. Heat the grill to 350F.
2. Position the grill rack 6 inches from the heat source.
3. Grill the steak for 10 minutes on each side or until slightly pink on the inside.
4. Meanwhile, prepare the sauce. In a small nonstick pan, water sauté the garlic, mushrooms, salt, pepper, and thyme for a minute. Pour in the broth and bring to a boil. Allow the sauce to simmer until the liquid is reduced.
5. Top the steaks with the mushroom sauce. Drizzle with olive oil.
6. Serve warm.

Nutrition Info:

- Info Per Servings 4.0g Carbs, 47.0g Protein, 36.0g Fat, 528 Calories

Beef And Egg Rice Bowls

Servings: 4

Cooking Time: 22 Minutes

Ingredients:

- 2 cups cauli rice
- 3 cups frozen mixed vegetables
- 3 tbsp ghee
- 1 lb skirt steak
- Salt and black pepper to taste
- 4 fresh eggs
- Hot sauce (sugar-free) for topping

Directions:

1. Mix the cauli rice and mixed vegetables in a bowl, sprinkle with a little water, and steam in the microwave for 1 minute to be tender. Share into 4 serving bowls.

2. Melt the ghee in a skillet, season the beef with salt and pepper, and brown for 5 minutes on each side. Use a perforated spoon to ladle the meat onto the vegetables.

3. Wipe out the skillet and return to medium heat, crack in an egg, season with salt and pepper and cook until the egg white has set, but the yolk is still runny 3 minutes. Remove egg onto the vegetable bowl and fry the remaining 3 eggs. Add to the other bowls.

4. Drizzle the beef bowls with hot sauce and serve.

Nutrition Info:

- Info Per Servings 4g Carbs, 15g Protein, 26g Fat, 320 Calories

Beef Bourguignon

Servings: 4

Cooking Time: 60 Minutes + Marinated Time

Ingredients:

- 3 tbsp coconut oil
- 1 tbsp dried parsley flakes
- 1 cup red wine
- 1 tsp dried thyme
- Salt and black pepper, to taste
- 1 bay leaf
- ⅓ cup coconut flour
- 2 lb beef, cubed
- 12 small white onions
- 4 pancetta slices, chopped
- 2 garlic cloves, minced
- ½ lb mushrooms, chopped

Directions:

1. In a bowl, combine the wine with bay leaf, olive oil, thyme, pepper, parsley, salt, and the beef cubes; set aside for 3 hours. Drain the meat, and reserve the marinade. Toss the flour over the meat to coat.

2. Heat a pan over medium-high heat, stir in the pancetta, and cook until slightly browned. Place in the onions and garlic, and cook for 3 minutes. Stir-fry in the meat and mushrooms for 4-5 minutes.

3. Pour in the marinade and 1 cup of water; cover and cook for 50 minutes. Season to taste and serve.

Nutrition Info:

- Info Per Servings 7g Carbs, 45g Protein, 26g Fat, 435 Calories

Beefy Bbq Ranch

Servings: 4
Cooking Time: 40 Minutes
Ingredients:

2-lbs London broil roast, sliced into 2-inch cubes
- 1 Hidden Valley Ranch seasoning mix packet
- 1-pound bacon
- 1 tablespoon barbecue powder
- 1 cup water

Pepper and salt to taste

Directions:

1. Add all ingredients in a pot on high fire and bring to a boil.
2. Once boiling, lower fire to a simmer and cook for 35 minutes.
3. Adjust seasoning to taste.
4. Serve and enjoy.

Nutrition Info:
- Info Per Servings 8.4g Carbs, 65.3g Protein, 39.7g Fat, 642 Calories

Grilled Sirloin Steak With Sauce Diane

Servings: 6
Cooking Time: 25 Minutes
Ingredients:
- Sirloin Steak
- 1 ½ lb sirloin steak
- Salt and black pepper to taste
- 1 tsp olive oil
- Sauce Diane
- 1 tbsp olive oil
- 1 clove garlic, minced
- 1 cup sliced porcini mushrooms
- 1 small onion, finely diced
- 2 tbsp butter
- 1 tbsp Dijon mustard
- 2 tbsp sugar-free Worcestershire sauce
- ¼ cup whiskey
- 2 cups double cream
- Salt and black pepper to taste

Directions:

1. Preheat the grill pan over high heat and as it heats, brush the steak with oil, sprinkle with salt and pepper, and rub the seasoning into the meat with your hands.
2. Cook the steak in the pan for 4 minutes on each side for medium rare and transfer to a chopping board to rest for 4 minutes before slicing. (Reserve the juice in the pan to season the sauce).
3. Heat the oil in a frying pan over medium heat and sauté the onion for 3 minutes. Add the butter, garlic, and mushrooms, and cook for 2 minutes.
4. Add the Worcestershire sauce, the reserved juice, and mustard. Stir and cook for 1 minute. Pour in the whiskey and cook further 1 minute until the sauce reduces by half. Swirl the pan and add the cream. Let it simmer to thicken for about 3 minutes. Adjust the taste with salt and pepper. Spoon the sauce over the steaks slices and serve with a side of celeriac mash.

Nutrition Info:
- Info Per Servings 2.9g Carbs, 36g Protein, 17g Fat, 434 Calories

Garlic Pork Chops With Mint Pesto

Servings: 4

Cooking Time: 3 Hours 10 Minutes

Ingredients:

- 1 cup parsley
- 1 cup mint
- 1½ onions, chopped
- ⅓ cup pistachios
- 1 tsp lemon zest
- 5 tbsp avocado oil
- Salt, to taste
- 4 pork chops
- 5 garlic cloves, minced
- Juice from 1 lemon

Directions:

1. In a food processor, combine the parsley with avocado oil, mint, pistachios, salt, lemon zest, and 1 onion. Rub the pork with this mixture, place in a bowl, and refrigerate for 1 hour while covered.
2. Remove the chops and set to a baking dish, place in ½ onion, and garlic; sprinkle with lemon juice, and bake for 2 hours in the oven at 250°F. Split amongst plates and enjoy.

Nutrition Info:

- Info Per Servings 5.5g Carbs, 37g Protein, 40g Fat, 567 Calories

Smoky Baby Back Ribs

Servings: 4

Cooking Time: 40 Minutes

Ingredients:

- 1 ½ teaspoon barbecue sauce
- 1 ½ teaspoon hoisin sauce
- ½ teaspoon smoked paprika
- 2 ½ pounds baby back ribs
- 1 cup water
- Pepper and salt to taste

Directions:

1. Add all ingredients in a pot on high fire and bring to a boil.
2. Once boiling, lower fire to a simmer and cook for 35 minutes.
3. Adjust seasoning to taste.
4. Serve and enjoy.

Nutrition Info:

- Info Per Servings 3.7g Carbs, 53.2g Protein, 55.0g Fat, 723 Calories

Lamb Stew With Veggies

Servings: 2
Cooking Time: 1 Hour 50 Minutes

Ingredients:

- 1 garlic clove, minced
- 1 parsnip, chopped
- 1 onion, chopped
- 1 tbsp olive oil
- 1 celery stalk, chopped
- 10 ounces lamb fillet, cut into pieces
- Salt and ground black pepper, to taste
- 1¼ cups vegetable stock
- 2 carrots, chopped
- ½ tbsp fresh rosemary, chopped
- 1 leek, chopped
- 1 tbsp mint sauce
- 1 tsp stevia
- 1 tbsp tomato puree
- ½ cauliflower, cut into florets
- ½ celeriac, chopped
- 2 tbsp butter

Directions:

1. Set the pot over medium heat and warm the oil, stir in the celery, onion, and garlic, and cook for 5 minutes. Stir in the lamb pieces, and cook for 3 minutes. Add in the stevia, carrot, parsnip, rosemary, mint sauce, stock, leek, tomato puree, boil the mixture, and cook for 1 hour and 30 minutes.

2. Meanwhile, heat a pot with water over medium heat, place in the celeriac, cover, and simmer for 10 minutes. Place in the cauliflower florets, cook for 15 minutes, drain everything, and combine with butter, pepper, and salt. Mash using a potato masher, and split the mash between 2 plates. Top with vegetable mixture and lamb and enjoy.

Nutrition Info:

- Info Per Servings 8.1g Carbs, 38g Protein, 42g Fat, 584 Calories

Beef With Grilled Vegetables

Servings: 4
Cooking Time: 30 Minutes

Ingredients:

- 4 sirloin steaks
- Salt and black pepper to taste
- 4 tbsp olive oil
- 3 tbsp balsamic vinegar
- Vegetables
- ½ lb asparagus, trimmed
- 1 cup green beans
- 1 cup snow peas
- 1 red bell peppers, seeded, cut into strips
- 1 orange bell peppers, seeded, cut into strips
- 1 medium red onion, quartered

Directions:

1. Set the grill pan over high heat and preheat it.

2. Grab 2 separate bowls; put the beef in one and the vegetables in another. Mix salt, pepper, olive oil, and balsamic vinegar in a small bowl, and pour half of the mixture over the beef and the other half over the vegetables. Coat the ingredients in both bowls with the sauce and cook the beef first.

3. Place the steaks in the grill pan and sear both sides for 2 minutes each, then continue cooking for 6 minutes on each side. When done, remove the beef onto a plate; set aside.

4. Now, pour the vegetables and marinade in the pan; and cook for 5 minutes, turning once.

5. Turn the heat off and share the vegetables into four plates. Top with each piece of beef, the sauce from the pan, and serve with a rutabaga mash.

Nutrition Info:

- Info Per Servings 5.6g Carbs, 66g Protein, 32.1g Fat, 515 Calories

Fish And Seafood Recipes

Yummy Shrimp Fried Rice

Servings: 6

Cooking Time: 20 Minutes

Ingredients:

- 4 tablespoons butter, divided
- 4 large eggs, lightly beaten
- 3 cups shredded cauliflower
- 1-pound uncooked medium shrimp, peeled and deveined
- 1/2 teaspoon salt
- 1/4 teaspoon pepper

Directions:

1. In a large skillet, melt 1 tablespoon butter over medium-high heat.

2. Pour eggs into skillet. As eggs set, lift edges, letting uncooked portion flow underneath. Remove eggs and keep warm.

3. Melt remaining butter in the skillet. Add the cauliflower, and shrimp; cook and stir for 5 minutes or until shrimp turn pink.

4. Meanwhile, chop eggs into small pieces. Return eggs to the pan; sprinkle with salt and pepper. Cook until heated through, stirring occasionally. Sprinkle with bacon if desired.

Nutrition Info:

- Info Per Servings 3.3g Carbs, 13g Protein, 11g Fat, 172 Calories

Parmesan Fish Bake

Servings: 4

Cooking Time: 40 Minutes

Ingredients:

- Cooking spray
- 2 salmon fillets, cubed
- 3 white fish, cubed
- 1 broccoli, cut into florets
- 1 tbsp butter, melted
- Pink salt and black pepper to taste
- 1 cup crème fraiche
- ¼ cup grated Parmesan cheese
- Grated Parmesan cheese for topping

Directions:

1. Preheat oven to 400ºF and grease an 8 x 8 inches casserole dish with cooking spray. Toss the fish cubes and broccoli in butter and season with salt and pepper to taste. Spread in the greased dish.

2. Mix the crème fraiche with Parmesan cheese, pour and smear the cream on the fish, and sprinkle with some more Parmesan. Bake for 25 to 30 minutes until golden brown on top, take the dish out, sit for 5 minutes and spoon into plates. Serve with lemon-mustard asparagus.

Nutrition Info:

- Info Per Servings 4g Carbs, 28g Protein, 17g Fat, 354 Calories

Steamed Cod With Ginger

Servings: 4

Cooking Time: 15 Minutes

Ingredients:

- 4 cod fillets, skin removed
- 3 tbsp. lemon juice, freshly squeezed
- 2 tbsp. coconut aminos
- 2 tbsp. grated ginger
- 6 scallions, chopped
- 5 tbsp coconut oil
- Pepper and salt to taste

Directions:

1. Place a trivet in a large saucepan and pour a cup or two of water into the pan. Bring to a boil.
2. In a small bowl, whisk well lemon juice, coconut aminos, coconut oil, and grated ginger.
3. Place scallions in a heatproof dish that fits inside a saucepan. Season scallions mon with pepper and salt. Drizzle with ginger mixture. Sprinkle scallions on top.
4. Seal dish with foil. Place the dish on the trivet inside the saucepan. Cover and steam for 15 minutes.
5. Serve and enjoy.

Nutrition Info:

Info Per Servings 10g Carbs, 28.3g Protein, 40g Fat, 514 Calories

Pistachio-crusted Salmon

Servings: 4

Cooking Time: 35 Minutes

Ingredients:

- 4 salmon fillets
- ½ tsp pepper
- 1 tsp salt
- ¼ cup mayonnaise
- ½ cup chopped pistachios
- Sauce
- 1 chopped shallot
- 2 tsp lemon zest
- 1 tbsp olive oil
- A pinch of pepper
- 1 cup heavy cream

Directions:

1. Preheat the oven to 370ºF.
2. Brush the salmon with mayonnaise and season with salt and pepper. Coat with pistachios, place in a lined baking dish and bake for 15 minutes.
3. Heat the olive oil in a saucepan and sauté the shallot for 3 minutes. Stir in the rest of the sauce ingredients. Bring the mixture to a boil and cook until thickened. Serve the fish with the sauce.

Nutrition Info:

- Info Per Servings 6g Carbs, 34g Protein, 47g Fat, 563 Calories

Seasoned Salmon With Parmesan

Servings: 4

Cooking Time: 20 Mins

Ingredients:

- 2 lbs. salmon fillet
- 3 minced garlic cloves
- ¼ cup. chopped parsley
- ½ cup. grated parmesan cheese
- Salt and pepper to taste

Directions:

1. Preheat oven to 425 degrees F. Line a baking sheet with parchment paper.
2. Lay salmon fillets on the lined baking sheet, season with salt and pepper to taste.
3. Bake for 10 minutes. Remove from the oven and sprinkle with garlic, parmesan and parsley.
4. Place in the oven to cook for 5 more minutes. Transfer to plates before serving.

Nutrition Info:

- Info Per Servings 0.6g Carbs, 25g Protein, 12g Fat, 210 Calories

Sour Cream Salmon With Parmesan

Servings: 4

Cooking Time: 25 Minutes

Ingredients:

- 1 cup sour cream
- ½ tbsp minced dill
- ½ lemon, zested and juiced
- Pink salt and black pepper to season
- 4 salmon steaks
- ½ cup grated Parmesan cheese

Directions:

1. Preheat oven to 400°F and line a baking sheet with parchment paper; set aside. In a bowl, mix the sour cream, dill, lemon zest juice, salt and pepper, and set aside.

2. Season the fish with salt and black pepper, drizzle lemon juice on both sides of the fish and arrange them in the baking sheet Spread the sour cream mixture on each fish and sprinkle with Parmesan.

3. Bake the fish for 15 minutes and after broil the top for 2 minutes with a close watch for a nice a brown color. Plate the fish and serve with buttery green beans.

Nutrition Info:

- Info Per Servings 1.2g Carbs, 16.2g Protein, 23.4g Fat, 288 Calories

Salmon Panzanella

Servings: 4

Cooking Time: 22 Minutes

Ingredients:

- 1 lb skinned salmon, cut into 4 steaks each
- 1 cucumber, peeled, seeded, cubed
- Salt and black pepper to taste
- 8 black olives, pitted and chopped
- 1 tbsp capers, rinsed
- 2 large tomatoes, diced
- 3 tbsp red wine vinegar
- ¼ cup thinly sliced red onion
- 3 tbsp olive oil
- 2 slices day-old zero carb bread, cubed
- ¼ cup thinly sliced basil leaves

Directions:

1. Preheat a grill to 350°F and prepare the salad. In a bowl, mix the cucumbers, olives, pepper, capers, tomatoes, wine vinegar onion, olive oil, bread, and basil leaves. Let sit for the flavors to incorporate.

2. Season the salmon steaks with salt and pepper; grill them on both sides for 8 minutes in total. Serve the salmon steaks warm on a bed of the veggies' salad.

Nutrition Info:

- Info Per Servings 3.1g Carbs, 28.5g Protein, 21.7g Fat, 338 Calories

Grilled Shrimp With Chimichurri Sauce

Servings: 4
Cooking Time: 55 Minutes
Ingredients:

- 1 pound shrimp, peeled and deveined
- 2 tbsp olive oil
- Juice of 1 lime
- Chimichurri
- ½ tsp salt
- ¼ cup olive oil
- 2 garlic cloves
- ¼ cup red onion, chopped
- ¼ cup red wine vinegar
- ½ tsp pepper
- 2 cups parsley
- ¼ tsp red pepper flakes

Directions:

1. Process the chimichurri ingredients in a blender until smooth; set aside. Combine shrimp, olive oil, and lime juice, in a bowl, and let marinate in the fridge for 30 minutes. Preheat your grill to medium. Add shrimp and cook about 2 minutes per side. Serve shrimp drizzled with the chimichurri sauce.

Nutrition Info:

- Info Per Servings 3.5g Carbs, 16g Protein, 20.3g Fat, 283 Calories

Coconut Crab Patties

Servings: 8
Cooking Time: 15 Minutes
Ingredients:

- 2 tbsp coconut oil
- 1 tbsp lemon juice
- 1 cup lump crab meat
- 2 tsp Dijon mustard
- 1 egg, beaten
- 1 ½ tbsp coconut flour

Directions:

1. In a bowl to the crabmeat add all the ingredients, except for the oil; mix well to combine. Make patties out of the mixture. Melt the coconut oil in a skillet over medium heat. Add the crab patties and cook for about 2-3 minutes per side.

Nutrition Info:

- Info Per Servings 3.6g Carbs, 15.3g Protein, 11.5g Fat, 215 Calories

Thyme-sesame Crusted Halibut

Servings: 2
Cooking Time: 15 Minutes
Ingredients:

- 8 oz. halibut, cut into 2 portions
- 1 tbsp. lemon juice, freshly squeezed
- 1 tsp. dried thyme leaves
- 1 tbsp. sesame seeds, toasted
- Salt and pepper to taste

Directions:

1. Place a trivet in a large saucepan and pour a cup or two of water into the pan. Bring it to a boil.
2. Place halibut in a heatproof dish that fits inside a saucepan. Season with lemon juice, salt, and pepper. Sprinkle with dried thyme leaves and sesame seeds.
3. Seal dish with foil. Place the dish on the trivet inside the saucepan. Cover and steam for 15 minutes.
4. Serve and enjoy.

Nutrition Info:

- Info Per Servings 4.2g Carbs, 17.5g Protein, 17.7g Fat, 246 Calories

Cilantro Shrimp

Servings: 4

Cooking Time: 10 Minutes

Ingredients:

- 1/2 cup reduced-fat Asian sesame salad dressing
- 1-pound uncooked shrimp, peeled and deveined
- Lime wedges
- 1/4 cup chopped fresh cilantro
- 5 tablespoon olive oil
- Salt and pepper

Directions:

1. In a large nonstick skillet, heat 1 tablespoon dressing over medium heat. Add shrimp; cook and stir 1 minute.
2. Stir in remaining dressing; cook, uncovered, until shrimp turn pink, 1-2 minutes longer.
3. To serve, squeeze lime juice over the top; sprinkle with cilantro, pepper, and salt. If desired, serve with rice.

Nutrition Info:

- Info Per Servings 4.7g Carbs, 32g Protein, 39g Fat, 509 Calories

Creamy Hoki With Almond Bread Crust

Servings: 4

Cooking Time: 50 Minutes

Ingredients:

- 1 cup flaked smoked hoki, bones removed
- 1 cup cubed hoki fillets, cubed
- 4 eggs
- 1 cup water
- 3 tbsp almond flour
- 1 medium white onion, sliced
- 2 cups sour cream
- 1 tbsp chopped parsley
- 1 cup pork rinds, crushed
- 1 cup grated cheddar cheese
- Salt and black pepper to taste
- Cooking spray

Directions:

1. Preheat the oven to 360ºF and lightly grease a baking dish with cooking spray.
2. Then, boil the eggs in water in a pot over medium heat to be well done for 12 minutes, run the eggs under cold water and peel the shells. After, place on a cutting board and chop them.
3. Melt the butter in a saucepan over medium heat and sauté the onion for about 4 minutes. Turn the heat off and stir the almond flour into it to form a roux. Turn the heat back on and cook the roux to be golden brown and stir in the cream until the mixture is smooth. Season with salt and pepper, and stir in the parsley.
4. Spread the smoked and cubed fish in the baking dish, sprinkle the eggs on top, and spoon the sauce over. In a bowl, mix the pork rinds with the cheddar cheese, and sprinkle it over the sauce.
5. Bake the casserole in the oven for 20 minutes until the top is golden and the sauce and cheese are bubbly. Remove the bake after and serve with a steamed green vegetable mix.

Nutrition Info:

- Info Per Servings 3.5g Carbs, 28.5g Protein, 27g Fat, 386 Calories

Seared Scallops With Chorizo And Asiago Cheese

Servings: 4

Cooking Time: 15 Minutes

Ingredients:

- 2 tbsp ghee
- 16 fresh scallops
- 8 ounces chorizo, chopped
- 1 red bell pepper, seeds removed, sliced
- 1 cup red onions, finely chopped
- 1 cup asiago cheese, grated
- Salt and black pepper to taste

Directions:

1. Melt half of the ghee in a skillet over medium heat, and cook the onion and bell pepper for 5 minutes until tender. Add the chorizo and stir-fry for another 3 minutes. Remove and set aside.

2. Pat dry the scallops with paper towels, and season with salt and pepper. Add the remaining ghee to the skillet and sear the scallops for 2 minutes on each side to have a golden brown color. Add the chorizo mixture back and warm through. Transfer to serving platter and top with asiago cheese.

Nutrition Info:

- Info Per Servings 5g Carbs, 36g Protein, 32g Fat, 491 Calories

Halibut En Papillote

Servings: 4

Cooking Time: 15 Minutes

Ingredients:

- 4 halibut fillets
- ½ tbsp. grated ginger
- 1 cup chopped tomatoes
- 1 shallot, thinly sliced
- 1 lemon
- 5 tbsp olive oil
- Salt and pepper to taste

Directions:

1. Slice lemon in half. Slice one lemon in circles.
2. Juice the other half of the lemon in a small bowl. Mix in grated ginger and season with pepper and salt.
3. Place a trivet in a large saucepan and pour a cup or two of water into the pan. Bring to a boil.
4. Get 4 large foil and place one fillet in the middle of each foil. Season with fillet salt and pepper. Drizzle with olive oil. Add the grated ginger, tomatoes, and shallots equally. Fold the foil to create a pouch and crimp the edges.
5. Place the foil containing the fish on the trivet. Cover saucepan and steam for 15 minutes.
6. Serve and enjoy in pouches.

Nutrition Info:

- Info Per Servings 2.7g Carbs, 20.3g Protein, 32.3g Fat, 410 Calories

Lemon Chili Halibut

Servings: 2
Cooking Time: 15 Minutes
Ingredients:

- 1-lb halibut fillets
- 1 lemon, sliced
- 1 tablespoon chili pepper flakes
- Pepper and salt to taste
- 4 tbsp olive oil

Directions:

1. In a heat-proof dish that fits inside saucepan, place fish. Top fish with chili flakes, lemon slices, salt, and pepper. Drizzle with olive oil. Cover dish with foil
2. Place a large saucepan on the medium-high fire. Place a trivet inside the saucepan and fill the pan halfway with water. Cover and bring to a boil.
3. Place dish on the trivet.
4. Cover pan and steam for 10 minutes. Let it rest in pan for another 5 minutes.
5. Serve and enjoy topped with pepper.

Nutrition Info:

- Info Per Servings 4.2g Carbs, 42.7g Protein, 58.4g Fat, 675 Calories

Cod With Balsamic Tomatoes

Servings: 4
Cooking Time: 30 Minutes
Ingredients:

- 4 center-cut bacon strips, chopped
- 4 cod fillets
- 2 cups grape tomatoes, halved
- 2 tablespoons balsamic vinegar
- 4 tablespoons olive oil
- 1/2 teaspoon salt
- 1/4 teaspoon pepper

Directions:

1. In a large skillet, heat olive oil and cook bacon over medium heat until crisp, stirring occasionally.
2. Remove with a slotted spoon; drain on paper towels.
3. Sprinkle fillets with salt and pepper. Add fillets to bacon drippings; cook over medium-high heat until fish just begins to flake easily with a fork, 4-6 minutes on each side. Remove and keep warm.
4. Add tomatoes to skillet; cook and stir until tomatoes are softened, 2-4 minutes. Stir in vinegar; reduce heat to medium-low. Cook until sauce is thickened, 1-2 minutes longer.
5. Serve cod with tomato mixture and bacon.

Nutrition Info:

- Info Per Servings 5g Carbs, 26g Protein, 30.4g Fat, 442 Calories

Buttery Almond Lemon Tilapia

Servings: 4
Cooking Time: 10 Minutes

Ingredients:

- 4 tilapia fillets
- 1/4 cup butter, cubed
- 1/4 cup white wine or chicken broth
- 2 tablespoons lemon juice
- 1/4 cup sliced almonds
- 1/2 teaspoon salt
- 1/4 teaspoon pepper
- 1 tablespoon olive oil

Directions:

1. Sprinkle fillets with salt and pepper. In a large nonstick skillet, heat oil over medium heat.
2. Add fillets; cook until fish just begins to flake easily with a fork, 2-3 minutes on each side. Remove and keep warm.
3. Add butter, wine and lemon juice to the same pan; cook and stir until butter is melted.
4. Serve with fish; sprinkle with almonds.

Nutrition Info:

- Info Per Servings 2g Carbs, 22g Protein, 19g Fat, 269 Calories

Simple Steamed Salmon Fillets

Servings: 3
Cooking Time: 15 Minutes

Ingredients:

- 10 oz. salmon fillets
- 2 tbsp. coconut aminos
- 2 tbsp. lemon juice, freshly squeezed
- 1 tsp. sesame seeds, toasted
- 3 tbsp sesame oil
- Salt and pepper to taste

Directions:

1. Place a trivet in a large saucepan and pour a cup or two of water into the pan. Bring to a boil.
2. Place salmon in a heatproof dish that fits inside the saucepan. Season salmon with pepper and salt. Drizzle with coconut aminos, lemon juice, sesame oil, and sesame seeds.
3. Seal dish with foil. Place the dish on the trivet inside the saucepan. Cover and steam for 15 minutes.
4. Serve and enjoy.

Nutrition Info:

- Info Per Servings 2.6g Carbs, 20.1g Protein, 17.4g Fat, 210 Calories

Blackened Fish Tacos With Slaw

Servings: 4
Cooking Time: 20 Minutes

Ingredients:

- 1 tbsp olive oil
- 1 tsp chili powder
- 2 tilapia fillets
- 1 tsp paprika
- 4 low carb tortillas
- Slaw:
- ½ cup red cabbage, shredded
- 1 tbsp lemon juice
- 1 tsp apple cider vinegar
- 1 tbsp olive oil

Directions:

1. Season the tilapia with chili powder and paprika. Heat the olive oil in a skillet over medium heat.
2. Add tilapia and cook until blackened, about 3 minutes per side. Cut into strips. Divide the tilapia between the tortillas. Combine all slaw ingredients in a bowl. Split the slaw among the tortillas.

Nutrition Info:

- Info Per Servings 3.5g Carbs, 13.8g Protein, 20g Fat, 268 Calories

Lemon Garlic Shrimp

Servings: 6

Cooking Time: 22 Minutes

Ingredients:

- ½ cup butter, divided
- 2 lb shrimp, peeled and deveined
- Pink salt and black pepper to taste
- ¼ tsp sweet paprika
- 1 tbsp minced garlic
- 3 tbsp water
- 1 lemon, zested and juiced
- 2 tbsp chopped parsley

Directions:

1. Melt half of the butter in a large skillet over medium heat, season the shrimp with salt, pepper, paprika, and add to the butter. Stir in the garlic and cook the shrimp for 4 minutes on both sides until pink. Remove to a bowl and set aside.

2. Put the remaining butter in the skillet; include the lemon zest, juice, and water. Cook until the butter has melted, about 1 minute. Add the shrimp, parsley, and adjust the taste with salt and black pepper. Cook for 2 minutes on low heat. Serve the shrimp and sauce with squash pasta.

Nutrition Info:

- Info Per Servings 2g Carbs, 13g Protein, 22g Fat, 258 Calories

Red Cabbage Tilapia Taco Bowl

Servings: 4

Cooking Time: 20 Minutes

Ingredients:

- 2 cups cauli rice
- Water for sprinkling
- 2 tsp ghee
- 4 tilapia fillets, cut into cubes
- ¼ tsp taco seasoning
- Pink salt and chili pepper to taste
- ¼ head red cabbage, shredded
- 1 ripe avocado, pitted and chopped

Directions:

1. Sprinkle cauli rice in a bowl with a little water and microwave for 3 minutes. Fluff after with a fork and set aside. Melt ghee in a skillet over medium heat, rub the tilapia with the taco seasoning, salt, and chili pepper, and fry until brown on all sides, for about 8 minutes in total.

2. Transfer to a plate and set aside. In 4 serving bowls, share the cauli rice, cabbage, fish, and avocado. Serve with chipotle lime sour cream dressing.

Nutrition Info:

- Info Per Servings 4g Carbs, 16.5g Protein, 23.4g Fat, 269 Calories

Chipotle Salmon Asparagus

Servings: 2

Cooking Time: 15 Minutes

Ingredients:

- 1-lb salmon fillet, skin on
- 2 teaspoon chipotle paste
- A handful of asparagus spears, trimmed
- 1 lemon, sliced thinly
- A pinch of rosemary
- Salt to taste
- 5 tbsp olive oil

Directions:

1. In a heat-proof dish that fits inside the saucepan, add asparagus spears on the bottom of the dish. Place fish, top with rosemary, and lemon slices. Season with chipotle paste and salt. Drizzle with olive oil. Cover dish with foil.
2. Place a large saucepan on the medium-high fire. Place a trivet inside the saucepan and fill the pan halfway with water. Cover and bring to a boil.
3. Place dish on the trivet.
4. Cover pan and steam for 10 minutes. Let it rest in pan for another 5 minutes.
5. Serve and enjoy topped with pepper.

Nutrition Info:

- Info Per Servings 2.8g Carbs, 35.0g Protein, 50.7g Fat, 651 Calories

Steamed Herbed Red Snapper

Servings: 4

Cooking Time: 15 Minutes

Ingredients:

- 4 red snapper fillets
- ¼ tsp. paprika
- 3 tbsp. lemon juice, freshly squeezed
- 1 ½ tsp chopped fresh herbs of your choice (rosemary, thyme, basil, or parsley)
- 6 tbsp olive oil
- Salt and pepper to taste

Directions:

1. In a small bowl, whisk well paprika, lemon juice, olive oil, and herbs. Season with pepper and salt.
2. Place a trivet in a large saucepan and pour a cup or two of water into the pan. Bring to a boil.
3. Place snapper in a heatproof dish that fits inside a saucepan. Season snapper with pepper and salt. Drizzle with lemon mixture.
4. Seal dish with foil. Place the dish on the trivet inside the saucepan. Cover and steam for 15 minutes.
5. Serve and enjoy.

Nutrition Info:

- Info Per Servings 2.1g Carbs, 45.6g Protein, 20.3g Fat, 374 Calories

Flounder With Dill And Capers

Servings: 4

Cooking Time: 15 Minutes

Ingredients:

- 4 flounder fillets
- 1 tbsp. chopped fresh dill
- 2 tbsp. capers, chopped
- 4 lemon wedges
- 6 tbsp olive oil
- Salt and pepper to taste

Directions:

1. Place a trivet in a large saucepan and pour a cup or two of water into the pan. Bring to a boil.
2. Place flounder in a heatproof dish that fits inside a saucepan. Season snapper with pepper and salt. Drizzle with olive oil on all sides. Sprinkle dill and capers on top of the filet.
3. Seal dish with foil. Place the dish on the trivet inside the saucepan. Cover and steam for 15 minutes.
4. Serve and enjoy with lemon wedges.

Nutrition Info:

- Info Per Servings 8.6g Carbs, 20.3g Protein, 35.9g Fat, 447 Calories

Simply Steamed Alaskan Cod

Servings: 2

Cooking Time: 15 Minutes

Ingredients:

- 1-lb fillet wild Alaskan Cod
- 1 cup cherry tomatoes, halved
- 1 tbsp balsamic vinegar
- 1 tbsp fresh basil chopped
- Salt and pepper to taste
- 5 tbsp olive oil

Directions:

1. In a heat-proof dish that fits inside the saucepan, add all ingredients except for basil. Mix well.
2. Place a large saucepan on the medium-high fire. Place a trivet inside the saucepan and fill pan halfway with water. Cover and bring to a boil.
3. Cover dish with foil and place on a trivet.
4. Cover pan and steam for 10 minutes. Let it rest in pan for another 5 minutes.
5. Serve and enjoy topped with fresh basil.

Nutrition Info:

- Info Per Servings 4.2g Carbs, 41.0g Protein, 36.6g Fat, 495.2 Calories

Alaskan Cod With Mustard Cream Sauce

Serves: 4

Cooking Time: 10 Minutes

Ingredients:

- 1 tablespoon coconut oil
- 4 Alaskan cod fillets
- Salt and freshly ground black pepper, to taste
- 6 leaves basil, chiffonade
- Mustard Cream Sauce:
- 1 teaspoon yellow mustard
- 1 teaspoon paprika
- 1/4 teaspoon ground bay leaf
- 3 tablespoons cream cheese
- 1/2 cup Greek-style yogurt
- 1 garlic clove, minced
- 1 teaspoon lemon zest
- 1 tablespoon fresh parsley, minced
- Sea salt and ground black pepper, to taste

Directions:

1. Heat coconut oil in a pan over medium heat. Sear the fish for 2 to 3 minutes per side. Season with salt and ground black pepper.
2. Mix all ingredients for the sauce until everything is well combined. Top the fish fillets with the sauce and serve garnished with fresh basil leaves. Bon appétit!

Nutrition Info:

- Per Serves 2.6g Carbs; 19.8g Protein; 8.2g Fat; 166 Calories;

Vegan, Vegetable & Meatless Recipes

Parmesan Roasted Cabbage

Servings: 4

Cooking Time: 25 Minutes

Ingredients:

- Cooking spray
- 1 large head green cabbage
- 4 tbsp melted butter
- 1 tsp garlic powder
- Salt and black pepper to taste
- 1 cup grated Parmesan cheese
- Grated Parmesan cheese for topping
- 1 tbsp chopped parsley to garnish

Directions:

1. Preheat oven to 400ºF, line a baking sheet with foil, and grease with cooking spray.

2. Stand the cabbage and run a knife from the top to bottom to cut the cabbage into wedges. Remove stems and wilted leaves. Mix the butter, garlic, salt, and black pepper until evenly combined.

3. Brush the mixture on all sides of the cabbage wedges and sprinkle with parmesan cheese.

4. Place on the baking sheet, and bake for 20 minutes to soften the cabbage and melt the cheese. Remove the cabbages when golden brown, plate and sprinkle with extra cheese and parsley. Serve warm with pan-glazed tofu.

Nutrition Info:

- Info Per Servings 4g Carbs, 17.5g Protein, 19.3g Fat, 268 Calories

Creamy Vegetable Stew

Servings: 4

Cooking Time: 32 Minutes

Ingredients:

- 2 tbsp ghee
- 1 tbsp onion garlic puree
- 4 medium carrots, peeled and chopped
- 1 large head cauliflower, cut into florets
- 2 cups green beans, halved
- Salt and black pepper to taste
- 1 cup water
- 1 ½ cups heavy cream

Directions:

1. Melt ghee in a saucepan over medium heat and sauté onion-garlic puree to be fragrant, 2 minutes.

2. Stir in carrots, cauliflower, and green beans, salt, and pepper, add the water, stir again, and cook the vegetables on low heat for 25 minutes to soften. Mix in the heavy cream to be incorporated, turn the heat off, and adjust the taste with salt and pepper. Serve the stew with almond flour bread.

Nutrition Info:

- Info Per Servings 6g Carbs, 8g Protein, 26.4g Fat, 310 Calories

Colorful Vegan Soup

Servings: 6
Cooking Time: 25 Minutes
Ingredients:

- 2 tsp olive oil
- 1 red onion, chopped
- 2 cloves garlic, minced
- 1 celery stalk, chopped
- 1 head broccoli, chopped
- 1 carrot, sliced
- 1 cup spinach, torn into pieces
- 1 cup collard greens, chopped
- Sea salt and black pepper, to taste
- 2 thyme sprigs, chopped
- 1 rosemary sprig, chopped
- 2 bay leaves
- 6 cups vegetable stock
- 2 tomatoes, chopped
- 1 cup almond milk
- 1 tbsp white miso paste
- ½ cup arugula

Directions:

1. Place a large pot over medium-high heat and warm oil. Add in carrots, celery, onion, broccoli, garlic, and sauté until soft.
2. Place in spinach, salt, rosemary, tomatoes, bay leaves, ground black pepper, collard greens, thyme, and vegetable stock. On low heat, simmer the mixture for 15 minutes while the lid is slightly open.
3. Stir in white miso paste, watercress, and almond milk and cook for 5 more minutes.

Nutrition Info:

- Info Per Servings 9g Carbs, 2.9g Protein, 11.4g Fat, 142 Calories

Parsnip Chips With Avocado Dip

Servings: 6
Cooking Time: 20 Minutes
Ingredients:

- 2 avocados, pitted
- 2 tsp lime juice
- Salt and black pepper, to taste
- 2 garlic cloves, minced
- 2 tbsp olive oil
- For Parsnip Chips
- 3 cups parsnips, sliced
- 1 tbsp olive oil
- Sea salt and garlic powder, to taste

Directions:

1. Use a fork to mash avocado pulp. Stir in fresh lime juice, pepper, 2 tbsp of olive oil, garlic, and salt until well combined. Remove to a bowl and set the oven to 300 ºF. Grease a baking sheet with spray.
2. Set parsnip slices on the baking sheet; toss with garlic powder, 1 tbsp of olive oil, and salt. Bake for 15 minutes until slices become dry. Serve alongside well-chilled avocado dip.

Nutrition Info:

- Info Per Servings 9.4g Carbs, 2.3g Protein, 26.7g Fat, 269 Calories

Vegan Mushroom Pizza

Servings: 4

Cooking Time: 35 Minutes

Ingredients:

- 2 tsp ghee
- 1 cup chopped button mushrooms
- ½ cup sliced mixed colored bell peppers
- Pink salt and black pepper to taste
- 1 almond flour pizza bread
- 1 cup tomato sauce
- 1 tsp vegan Parmesan cheese
- Vegan Parmesan cheese for garnish

Directions:

1. Melt ghee in a skillet over medium heat, sauté the mushrooms and bell peppers for 10 minutes to soften. Season with salt and black pepper. Turn the heat off.
2. Put the pizza bread on a pizza pan, spread the tomato sauce all over the top and scatter vegetables evenly on top. Season with a little more salt and sprinkle with parmesan cheese.
3. Bake for 20 minutes until the vegetables are soft and the cheese has melted and is bubbly. Garnish with extra parmesan cheese. Slice pizza and serve with chilled berry juice.

Nutrition Info:

- Info Per Servings 8g Carbs, 15g Protein, 20g Fat, 295 Calories

Herb Butter With Parsley

Servings: 1

Cooking Time: 0 Minutes

Ingredients:

- 5 oz. butter, at room temperature
- 1 garlic clove, pressed
- ½ tbsp garlic powder
- 4 tbsp fresh parsley, finely chopped
- 1 tsp lemon juice
- ½ tsp salt

Directions:

1. In a bowl, stir all ingredients until completely combined. Set aside for 15 minutes or refrigerate it before serving.

Nutrition Info:

- Info Per Servings 1g Carbs, 1g Protein, 28g Fat, 258 Calories

Creamy Kale And Mushrooms

Servings: 3

Cooking Time: 15 Minutes

Ingredients:

- 3 cloves of garlic, minced
- 1 onion, chopped
- 1 bunch kale, stems removed and leaves chopped
- 3 white button mushrooms, chopped
- 1 cup heavy cream
- 5 tablespoons oil
- Salt and pepper to taste

Directions:

1. Heat oil in a pot.
2. Sauté the garlic and onion until fragrant for 2 minutes.
3. Stir in mushrooms. Season with pepper and salt. Cook for 8 minutes.
4. Stir in kale and coconut milk. Simmer for 5 minutes.
5. Adjust seasoning to taste.

Nutrition Info:

- Info Per Servings 7.9g Carbs, 6.0g Protein, 35.5g Fat, 365 Calories

Cauliflower Mash

Servings: 4

Cooking Time: 10 Minutes

Ingredients:

- 1 head of cauliflower
- ¼ tsp, garlic powder
- 1 handful of chives, chopped
- What you'll need from the store cupboard:
- ¼ tsp, salt
- ¼ tsp, ground black pepper

Directions:

1. Bring a pot of water to boil.
2. Chop cauliflower into florets. Place in a pot of boiling water and boil for 5 minutes.
3. Drain well.
4. Place florets in a blender. Add remaining ingredients except for chives and pulse to desired consistency.
5. Transfer to a bowl and toss in chives.
6. Serve and enjoy.

Nutrition Info:

- Info Per Servings 3.7g Carbs, 1.3g Protein, 0.2g Fat, 18 Calories

Zucchini Noodles

Servings: 6

Cooking Time: 15 Mins

Ingredients:

- 2 cloves garlic, minced
- 2 medium zucchini, cut into noodles with a spiralizer
- 12 zucchini blossoms, pistils removed; cut into strips
- 6 fresh basil leaves, cut into strips, or to taste
- 4 tablespoons olive oil
- Salt to taste

Directions:

1. In a large skillet over low heat, cook garlic in olive oil for 10 minutes until slightly browned. Add in zucchini and zucchin blossoms, stir well.
2. Toss in green beans and season with salt to taste; sprinkle with basil and serve.

Nutrition Info:

- Info Per Servings 13.5g Carbs, 5.7g Protein, 28.1g Fat, 348 Calories

Sautéed Celeriac With Tomato Sauce

Servings: 4
Cooking Time: 20 Minutes
Ingredients:

- 2 tbsp olive oil
- 1 garlic clove, crushed
- 1 celeriac, sliced
- ¼ cup vegetable stock
- Sea salt and black pepper, to taste
- For the Sauce
- 2 tomatoes, halved

- 2 tbsp olive oil
- ½ cup onions, chopped
- 2 cloves garlic, minced
- 1 chili, minced
- 1 bunch fresh basil, chopped
- 1 tbsp fresh cilantro, chopped
- Salt and black pepper, to taste

Directions:

1. Set a pan over medium-high heat and warm olive oil. Add in garlic and sauté for 1 minute. Stir in celeriac slices, stock and cook until softened. Sprinkle with black pepper and salt; kill the heat. Brush olive oil to the tomato halves. Microwave for 15 minutes; get rid of any excess liquid.
2. Remove the cooked tomatoes to a food processor; add the rest of the ingredients for the sauce and puree to obtain the desired consistency. Serve the celeriac topped with tomato sauce.

Nutrition Info:

- Info Per Servings 3g Carbs, 0.9g Protein, 13.6g Fat, 135 Calories

Endives Mix With Lemon Dressing

Servings: 8
Cooking Time: 0 Minutes
Ingredients:

- 1 bunch watercress
- 2 heads endive, halved lengthwise and thinly sliced
- 1 cup pomegranate seeds
- 1 shallot, thinly sliced

- 2 lemons, juiced and zested
- 1/4 teaspoon salt
- 1/8 teaspoon pepper
- 1/4 cup olive oil

Directions:

1. In a large bowl, combine watercress, endive, pomegranate seeds, and shallot.
2. In a small bowl, whisk the lemon juice, zest, salt, pepper, and olive oil. Drizzle over salad; toss to coat.

Nutrition Info:

- Info Per Servings 6g Carbs, 2g Protein, 13g Fat, 151 Calories

Grilled Spicy Eggplant

Servings: 2
Cooking Time: 20 Minutes
Ingredients:

- 2 small eggplants, cut into 1/2-inch slices
- 1/4 cup olive oil
- 2 tablespoons lime juice
- 3 teaspoons Cajun seasoning
- Salt and pepper to taste

Directions:

1. Brush eggplant slices with oil. Drizzle with lime juice; sprinkle with Cajun seasoning. Let stand for 5 minutes.
2. Grill eggplant, covered, over medium heat or broil 4 minutes. from heat until tender, 4-5 minutes per side.
3. Season with pepper and salt to taste.
4. Serve and enjoy.

Nutrition Info:

- Info Per Servings 7g Carbs, 5g Protein, 28g Fat, 350 Calories

Briam With Tomato Sauce

Servings: 4

Cooking Time: 70 Minutes

Ingredients:

- 3 tbsp olive oil
- 1 large eggplant, halved and sliced
- 1 large onion, thinly sliced
- 3 cloves garlic, sliced
- 5 tomatoes, diced
- 3 rutabagas, peeled and diced
- 1 cup sugar-free tomato sauce
- 4 zucchinis, sliced
- ¼ cup water
- Salt and black pepper to taste
- 1 tbsp dried oregano
- 2 tbsp chopped parsley

Directions:

1. Preheat the oven to 400ºF. Heat the olive oil in a skillet over medium heat and cook the eggplants in it for 6 minutes to brown on the edges. After, remove to a medium bowl.

2. Sauté the onion and garlic in the oil for 3 minutes and add them to the eggplants. Turn the heat off.

3. In the eggplants bowl, mix in the tomatoes, rutabagas, tomato sauce, and zucchinis. Add the water and stir in the salt, pepper, oregano, and parsley. Pour the mixture in the casserole dish. Place the dish in the oven and bake for 45 to 60 minutes. Serve the briam warm on a bed of cauli rice.

Nutrition Info:

- Info Per Servings 12.5g Carbs, 11.3g Protein, 12g Fat, 365 Calories

Grilled Parmesan Eggplant

Servings: 4

Cooking Time: 15 Minutes

Ingredients:

- 1 medium-sized eggplant
- 1 log fresh mozzarella cheese, cut into sixteen slices
- 1 small tomato, cut into eight slices
- 1/2 cup shredded Parmesan cheese
- Chopped fresh basil or parsley
- 1/2 teaspoon salt
- 1 tablespoon olive oil
- 1/2 teaspoon pepper

Directions:

1. Trim ends of the eggplant; cut eggplant crosswise into eight slices. Sprinkle with salt; let stand 5 minutes.

2. Blot eggplant dry with paper towels; brush both sides with oil and sprinkle with pepper. Grill, covered, over medium heat 4-6 minutes on each side or until tender. Remove from grill.

3. Top eggplant with mozzarella cheese, tomato, and Parmesan cheese. Grill, covered, 1-2 minutes longer or until cheese begins to melt. Top with basil.

Nutrition Info:

- Info Per Servings 10g Carbs, 26g Protein, 31g Fat, 449 Calories

Coconut Cauliflower & Parsnip Soup

Servings: 4

Cooking Time: 20 Minutes

Ingredients:

- 4 cups vegetable broth
- 2 heads cauliflower, cut into florets
- 1 cup parsnip, chopped
- 1 tbsp coconut oil
- 1 cup coconut milk
- ½ tsp red pepper flakes

Directions:

1. Add water in a pot set over medium-high heat and bring to a boil. Add in cauliflower florets and parsnip, cook for about 10 minutes. Add in broth and coconut oil. While on low heat, cook for an additional 5 minutes. Transfer the mixture to an immersion blender and puree.

2. Plate into four separate soup bowls; decorate each with red pepper flakes. Serve while warm.

Nutrition Info:

- Info Per Servings 7g Carbs, 2.7g Protein, 7.2g Fat, 94 Calories

Herbed Portobello Mushrooms

Servings: 2

Cooking Time: 10 Minutes

Ingredients:

- 2 Portobello mushrooms, stemmed and wiped clean
- 1 tsp minced garlic
- ¼ tsp dried rosemary
- 1 tablespoon balsamic vinegar
- ¼ cup grated provolone cheese
- 4 tablespoons olive oil
- Salt and pepper to taste

Directions:

1. In an oven, position rack 4-inches away from the top and preheat broiler.
2. Prepare a baking dish by spraying with cooking spray lightly.
3. Stemless, place mushroom gill side up.
4. Mix well garlic, rosemary, balsamic vinegar, and olive oil in a small bowl. Season with salt and pepper to taste.
5. Drizzle over mushrooms equally.
6. Marinate for at least 5 minutes before popping into the oven and broiling for 4 minutes per side or until tender.
7. Once cooked, remove from oven, sprinkle cheese, return to broiler and broil for a minute or two or until cheese melts.
8. Remove from oven and serve right away.

Nutrition Info:

- Info Per Servings 21.5g Carbs, 8.6g Protein, 5.1g Fat, 168 Calories

Tasty Cauliflower Dip

Servings: 4

Cooking Time: 10 Minutes

Ingredients:

- ¾ pound cauliflower, cut into florets
- ¼ cup olive oil
- Salt and black pepper, to taste
- 1 garlic clove, smashed
- 1 tbsp sesame paste
- 1 tbsp fresh lime juice
- ½ tsp garam masala

Directions:

1. Steam cauliflower until tender for 7 minutes in. Transfer to a blender and pulse until you attain a rice-like consistency.

2. Place in Garam Masala, oil, black paper, fresh lime juice, garlic, salt, and sesame paste. Blend the mixture until well combined. Decorate with some additional olive oil and serve. Otherwise, refrigerate until ready to use.

Nutrition Info:

- Info Per Servings 4.7g Carbs, 3.7g Protein, 8.2g Fat, 100 Calories

Onion & Nuts Stuffed Mushrooms

Servings: 4

Cooking Time: 30 Minutes

Ingredients:

- 1 tbsp sesame oil
- 1 onion, chopped
- 1 garlic clove, minced
- 1 pound mushrooms, stems removed
- Salt and black pepper, to taste
- ¼ cup raw pine nuts
- 2 tbsp parsley, chopped

Directions:

1. Set oven to 360ºF. Use a nonstick cooking spray to grease a large baking sheet. Into a frying pan, add sesame oil and warm. Place in garlic and onion and cook until soft.

2. Chop the mushroom stems and cook until tender. Turn off the heat, sprinkle with pepper and salt; add in pine nuts. Take the nut/mushroom mixture and stuff them to the mushroom caps and set on the baking sheet.

3. Bake the stuffed mushrooms for 30 minutes and remove to a wire rack to cool slightly. Add fresh parsley for garnish and serve.

Nutrition Info:

- Info Per Servings 7.4g Carbs, 4.8g Protein, 11.2g Fat, 139 Calories

Strawberry Mug Cake

Servings: 8

Cooking Time: 3 Mins

Ingredients:

- 2 slices fresh strawberry
- 1 teaspoon chia seeds
- 1 teaspoon poppy seeds
- What you'll need from the store cupboard:
- 1/4 teaspoon baking powder
- 3 leaves fresh mint
- 2 tablespoons cream of coconut

Directions:

1. Add all the ingredients together in a mug, stir until finely combined.

2. Cook in microwave at full power for 3 minutes then allow to cool before you serve.

Nutrition Info:

- Info Per Servings 4.7g Carbs, 2.4g Protein, 12g Fat, 196 Calories

Pumpkin Bake

Servings: 6

Cooking Time: 45 Minutes

Ingredients:

- 3 large Pumpkins, peeled and sliced
- 1 cup almond flour
- 1 cup grated mozzarella cheese
- 2 tbsp olive oil
- ½ cup chopped parsley

Directions:

1. Preheat the oven to 350ºF. Arrange the pumpkin slices in a baking dish, drizzle with olive oil, and bake for 35 minutes. Mix the almond flour, cheese, and parsley and when the pumpkin is ready, remove it from the oven, and sprinkle the cheese mixture all over. Place back in the oven and grill the top for 5 minutes.

Nutrition Info:

- Info Per Servings 5.7g Carbs, 2.7g Protein, 4.8g Fat, 125 Calories

Morning Coconut Smoothie

Servings: 4
Cooking Time: 5 Minutes
Ingredients:

- ½ cup water
- 1 ½ cups coconut milk
- 1 cup frozen cherries
- 4 cup fresh blueberries
- ¼ tsp vanilla extract
- 1 tbsp vegan protein powder

Directions:

1. Using a blender, combine all the ingredients and blend well until you attain a uniform and creamy consistency. Divide in glasses and serve!

Nutrition Info:

- Info Per Servings 14.9g Carbs, 2.6g Protein, 21.7g Fat, 247 Calories

Cremini Mushroom Stroganoff

Servings: 4
Cooking Time: 15 Minutes
Ingredients:

- 3 tbsp butter
- 1 white onion, chopped
- 4 cups cremini mushrooms, cubed
- 2 cups water
- ½ cup heavy cream
- ½ cup grated Parmesan cheese
- 1 ½ tbsp dried mixed herbs
- Salt and black pepper to taste

Directions:

1. Melt the butter in a saucepan over medium heat, sauté the onion for 3 minutes until soft.
2. Stir in the mushrooms and cook until tender, about 3 minutes. Add the water, mix, and bring to boil for 4 minutes until the water reduces slightly.
3. Pour in the heavy cream and parmesan cheese. Stir to melt the cheese. Also, mix in the dried herbs. Season with salt and pepper, simmer for 40 seconds and turn the heat off.
4. Ladle stroganoff over a bed of spaghetti squash and serve.

Nutrition Info:

- Info Per Servings 1g Carbs, 5g Protein, 28g Fat, 284 Calories

Grilled Cheese The Keto Way

Servings: 1
Cooking Time: 15 Minutes
Ingredients:

- 2 eggs
- ½ tsp baking powder
- 2 tbsp butter
- 2 tbsp almond flour
- 1 ½ tbsp psyllium husk powder
- 2 ounces cheddar cheese

Directions:

1. Whisk together all ingredients except 1 tbsp. butter and cheddar cheese. Place in a square oven-proof bowl, and microwave for 90 seconds. Flip the bun over and cut in half.
2. Place the cheddar cheese on one half of the bun and top with the other. Melt the remaining butter in a skillet. Add the sandwich and grill until the cheese is melted and the bun is crispy.

Nutrition Info:

- Info Per Servings 6.1g Carbs, 25g Protein, 51g Fat, 623 Calories

Zoodles With Avocado & Olives

Servings: 4

Cooking Time: 15 Minutes

Ingredients:

- 4 zucchinis, julienned or spiralized
- ½ cup pesto
- 2 avocados, sliced
- 1 cup kalamata olives, chopped
- ¼ cup chopped basil
- 2 tbsp olive oil
- ¼ cup chopped sun-dried tomatoes

Directions:

1. Heat half of the olive oil in a pan over medium heat. Add zoodles and cook for 4 minutes. Transfer to a plate. Stir in pesto, basil, salt, tomatoes, and olives. Top with avocado slices.

Nutrition Info:

- Info Per Servings 8.4g Carbs, 6.3g Protein, 42g Fat, 449 Calories

Avocado And Tomato Burritos

Servings: 4

Cooking Time: 5 Minutes

Ingredients:

- 2 cups cauli rice
- Water for sprinkling
- 6 zero carb flatbread
- 2 cups sour cream sauce
- 1 ½ cups tomato herb salsa
- 2 avocados, peeled, pitted, sliced

Directions:

1. Pour the cauli rice in a bowl, sprinkle with water, and soften in the microwave for 2 minutes.

2. On flatbread, spread the sour cream all over and distribute the salsa on top. Top with cauli rice and scatter the avocado evenly on top. Fold and tuck the burritos and cut into two.

Nutrition Info:

- Info Per Servings 6g Carbs, 8g Protein, 25g Fat, 303 Calories

Lemon Cauliflower "couscous" With Halloumi

Servings: 4

Cooking Time: 5 Minutes

Ingredients:

- 4 oz halloumi, sliced
- Cooking spray
- 1 cauliflower head, cut into small florets
- ¼ cup chopped cilantro
- ¼ cup chopped parsley
- ¼ chopped mint
- ½ lemon juiced
- Salt and black pepper to taste
- Sliced avocado to garnish

Directions:

1. Place a non-stick skillet over medium heat and lightly grease it with cooking spray.

2. Add the halloumi and fry for 2 minutes on each side to be golden brown, set aside. Turn the heat off.

3. Next, pour the cauli florets in a bowl and steam in the microwave for 2 minutes. They should be slightly cooked but crunchy. Remove the bowl from the microwave and let the cauli cool. Stir in the cilantro, parsley, mint, lemon juice, salt, and pepper.

4. Garnish the couscous with avocado slices and serve with grilled halloumi and vegetable sauce.

Nutrition Info:

- Info Per Servings 2.1g Carbs, 12g Protein, 15.6g Fat, 185 Calories

Soups, Stew & Salads Recipes

Watermelon And Cucumber Salad

Servings: 10
Cooking Time: 0 Minutes
Ingredients:

- ½ large watermelon, diced
- 1 cucumber, peeled and diced
- 1 red onion, chopped
- ¼ cup feta cheese
- ½ cup heavy cream
- Salt to taste
- 5 tbsp MCT or coconut oil

Directions:

1. Place all ingredients in a bowl.
2. Toss everything to coat.
3. Place in the fridge to cool before serving.

Nutrition Info:

- Info Per Servings 2.5g Carbs, 0.9g Protein, 100g Fat, 910 Calories

Traditional Greek Salad

Servings: 4
Cooking Time: 10 Minutes
Ingredients:

- 5 tomatoes, chopped
- 1 large cucumber, chopped
- 1 green bell pepper, chopped
- 1 small red onion, chopped
- 16 kalamata olives, chopped
- 4 tbsp capers
- 1 cup feta cheese, chopped
- 1 tsp oregano, dried
- 4 tbsp olive oil
- Salt to taste

Directions:

1. Place tomatoes, bell pepper, cucumber, onion, feta cheese and olives in a bowl; mix to combine well. Season with salt.
Combine capers, olive oil, and oregano, in a small bowl. Drizzle with the dressing to serve.

Nutrition Info:

- Info Per Servings 8g Carbs, 9.3g Protein, 28g Fat, 323 Calories

Mushroom Soup

Servings: 8
Cooking Time: 35 Minutes
Ingredients:

- 1-pound baby portobello mushrooms, chopped
- 2 tablespoons olive oil
- 1 carton reduced-sodium beef broth
- 2 cups heavy whipping cream
- 4 tablespoons butter
- 1/2 cup water

Directions:

1. In a Dutch oven, sauté mushrooms in oil and butter until tender.
2. Add the contents of seasoning packets, broth, and water. Bring to a boil.
3. Reduce heat; cover and simmer for 25 minutes.
4. Add cream and heat through.

Nutrition Info:

- Info Per Servings 3.6g Carbs, 8g Protein, 26g Fat, 280 Calories

Green Salad With Bacon And Blue Cheese

Servings: 4

Cooking Time: 15 Minutes

Ingredients:

- 2 pack mixed salad greens
- 8 strips bacon
- 1 ½ cups crumbled blue cheese
- 1 tbsp white wine vinegar
- 3 tbsp extra virgin olive oil
- Salt and black pepper to taste

Directions:

1. Pour the salad greens in a salad bowl; set aside. Fry bacon strips in a skillet over medium heat for 6 minutes, until browned and crispy. Chop the bacon and scatter over the salad. Add in half of the cheese, toss and set aside.

2. In a small bowl, whisk the white wine vinegar, olive oil, salt, and black pepper until dressing is well combined. Drizzle half of the dressing over the salad, toss, and top with remaining cheese. Divide salad into four plates and serve with crusted chicken frie along with remaining dressing.

Nutrition Info:

- Info Per Servings 2g Carbs, 4g Protein, 20g Fat, 205 Calories

Arugula Prawn Salad With Mayo Dressing

Servings: 4

Cooking Time: 15 Minutes

Ingredients:

- 4 cups baby arugula
- ½ cup garlic mayonnaise
- 3 tbsp olive oil
- 1 lb tiger prawns, peeled and deveined
- 1 tsp Dijon mustard
- Salt and chili pepper to season
- 2 tbsp lemon juice

Directions:

1. Add the mayonnaise, lemon juice and mustard in a small bowl. Mix until smooth and creamy. Heat 2 tbps of olive oil in a skillet over medium heat, add the prawns, season with salt, and chili pepper, and fry in the oil for 3 minutes on each side until prawns are pink. Set aside to a plate.

2. Place the arugula in a serving bowl and pour half of the dressing on the salad. Toss with 2 spoons until mixed, and add the remaining dressing. Divide salad into 4 plates and serve with prawns.

Nutrition Info:

- Info Per Servings 2g Carbs, 8g Protein, 20.3g Fat, 215 Calories

Creamy Cauliflower Soup With Bacon Chips

Servings: 4

Cooking Time: 25 Minutes

Ingredients:

- 2 tbsp ghee
- 1 onion, chopped
- 2 head cauliflower, cut into florets
- 2 cups water
- Salt and black pepper to taste
- 3 cups almond milk
- 1 cup shredded white cheddar cheese
- 3 bacon strips

Directions:

1. Melt the ghee in a saucepan over medium heat and sauté the onion for 3 minutes until fragrant.
2. Include the cauli florets, sauté for 3 minutes to slightly soften, add the water, and season with salt and black pepper. Bring to a boil, and then reduce the heat to low. Cover and cook for 10 minutes.
3. Puree cauliflower with an immersion blender until the ingredients are evenly combined and stir in the almond milk and cheese until the cheese melts. Adjust taste with salt and black pepper.
4. In a non-stick skillet over high heat, fry the bacon, until crispy. Divide soup between serving bowls, top with crispy bacon, and serve hot.

Nutrition Info:

- Info Per Servings 6g Carbs, 8g Protein, 37g Fat, 402 Calories

Pumpkin & Meat Peanut Stew

Servings: 6

Cooking Time: 45 Minutes

Ingredients:

- 1 cup pumpkin puree
- 2 pounds chopped pork stew meat
- 1 tbsp peanut butter
- 4 tbsp chopped peanuts
- 1 garlic clove, minced
- ½ cup chopped onion
- ½ cup white wine
- 1 tbsp olive oil
- 1 tsp lemon juice
- ¼ cup granulated sweetener
- ¼ tsp cardamom
- ¼ tsp allspice
- 2 cups water
- 2 cups chicken stock

Directions:

1. Heat the olive oil in a large pot and sauté onion for 3 minutes, until translucent. Add garlic and cook for 30 more seconds. Add the pork and cook until browned, about 5-6 minutes, stirring occasionally. Pour in the wine and cook for one minute.
2. Add in the remaining ingredients, except for the lemon juice and peanuts. Bring the mixture to a boil, and cook for 5 minutes. Reduce the heat to low, cover the pot, and let cook for about 30 minutes. Adjust seasoning and stir in the lemon juice before serving.
3. Ladle into serving bowls and serve topped with peanuts.

Nutrition Info:

- Info Per Servings 4g Carbs, 27.5g Protein, 33g Fat, 451 Calories

Beef Reuben Soup

Servings: 6

Cooking Time: 20 Minutes

Ingredients:

- 1 onion, diced
- 6 cups beef stock
- 1 tsp caraway seeds
- 2 celery stalks, diced
- 2 garlic cloves, minced
- 2 cups heavy cream
- 1 cup sauerkraut
- 1 pound corned beef, chopped
- 3 tbsp butter
- 1 ½ cup swiss cheese
- Salt and black pepper, to taste

Directions:

1. Melt the butter in a large pot. Add onion and celery, and fry for 3 minutes until tender. Add garlic and cook for another minute
2. Pour the beef stock over and stir in sauerkraut, salt, caraway seeds, and add a pinch of pepper. Bring to a boil. Reduce the heat to low, and add the corned beef. Cook for about 15 minutes, adjust the seasoning. Stir in heavy cream and cheese and cook for 1 minute.

Nutrition Info:

- Info Per Servings 8g Carbs, 23g Protein, 37g Fat, 450 Calories

Creamy Cauliflower Soup With Chorizo Sausage

Servings: 4

Cooking Time: 40 Minutes

Ingredients:

- 1 cauliflower head, chopped
- 1 turnip, chopped
- 3 tbsp butter
- 1 chorizo sausage, sliced
- 2 cups chicken broth
- 1 small onion, chopped
- 2 cups water
- Salt and black pepper, to taste

Directions:

1. Melt 2 tbsp. of the butter in a large pot over medium heat. Stir in onion and cook until soft and golden, about 3-4 minutes. Add cauliflower and turnip, and cook for another 5 minutes.
2. Pour the broth and water over. Bring to a boil, simmer covered, and cook for about 20 minutes until the vegetables are tender. Remove from heat. Melt the remaining butter in a skillet. Add the chorizo sausage and cook for 5 minutes until crispy. Puree the soup with a hand blender until smooth. Taste and adjust the seasonings. Serve the soup in deep bowls topped with the chorizo sausage.

Nutrition Info:

- Info Per Servings 5.7g Carbs, 10g Protein, 19.1g Fat, 251 Calories

Bacon Chowder

Servings: 6

Cooking Time: 15 Minutes

Ingredients:

- 1-pound bacon strips, chopped
- 1/4 cup chopped onion
- 1 can evaporated milk
- 1 sprig parsley, chopped
- 5 tablespoons butter
- 1/4 teaspoon salt
- 1/4 teaspoon pepper

Directions:

1. In a large skillet, cook bacon over medium heat until crisp, stirring occasionally. Remove with a slotted spoon; drain on paper towels. Discard drippings, reserving 1-1/2 teaspoons in the pan. Add onion to drippings; cook and stir over medium-high heat until tender.
2. Meanwhile, place all ingredients Bring to a boil over high heat. Reduce heat to medium; cook, uncovered, 10-15 minutes or until tender. Reserve 1 cup potato water.
3. Add milk, salt and pepper to the saucepan; heat through. Stir in bacon and onion.

Nutrition Info:

- Info Per Servings 5.4g Carbs, 10g Protein, 31.9g Fat, 322 Calories

Bacon And Pea Salad

Servings: 6

Cooking Time: 5 Minutes

Ingredients:

- 4 bacon strips
- 2 cups fresh peas
- ½ cup shredded cheddar cheese
- ½ cup ranch salad dressing
- 1/3 cup chopped red onions
- Salt and pepper to taste
- 3 tablespoons olive oil

Directions:

1. Heat skillet over medium flame and fry the bacon until crispy or until the fat has rendered. Transfer into a plate lined with a paper towel and crumble.
2. In a bowl, combine the rest of the ingredients and toss to coat.
3. Add in the bacon bits last.

Nutrition Info:

- Info Per Servings 2.9g Carbs, 3.5g Protein, 20.4g Fat, 205 Calories

Shrimp With Avocado & Cauliflower Salad

Servings: 6

Cooking Time: 30 Minutes

Ingredients:

- 1 cauliflower head, florets only
- 1 pound medium shrimp
- ¼ cup + 1 tbsp olive oil
- 1 avocado, chopped
- 3 tbsp chopped dill
- ¼ cup lemon juice
- 2 tbsp lemon zest
- Salt and black pepper to taste

Directions:

1. Heat 1 tbsp olive oil in a skillet and cook the shrimp until opaque, about 8-10 minutes. Place the cauliflower florets in a microwave-safe bowl, and microwave for 5 minutes. Place the shrimp, cauliflower, and avocado in a large bowl.
2. Whisk together the remaining olive oil, lemon zest, juice, dill, and some salt and pepper, in another bowl. Pour the dressing over, toss to combine and serve immediately.

Nutrition Info:

- Info Per Servings 5g Carbs, 15g Protein, 17g Fat, 214 Calories

Quail Eggs And Winter Melon Soup

Servings: 6

Cooking Time: 40 Minutes

Ingredients:

- 1-pound pork bones
- 4 cloves of garlic, minced
- 1 onion, chopped
- 1 winter melon, peeled and sliced
- 10 quail eggs, pre-boiled and peeled
- Pepper and salt to taste
- 6 cups water, divided
- Chopped cilantro for garnish (optional)

Directions:

1. Place a heavy-bottomed pot on medium-high fire.
2. Add 5 cups water and pork bones. Season generously with pepper.
3. Bring to a boil, lower fire to a simmer, cover and cook for 30 minutes. Discard bones.
4. Add remaining ingredients except for the cilantro. Cover and simmer for another 10 minutes.
5. Adjust seasoning to taste.
6. Serve and enjoy with cilantro for garnish.

Nutrition Info:

- Info Per Servings 5.6g Carbs, 4.0g Protein, 3.0g Fat, 65 Calories

Garlic Chicken Salad

Servings: 4

Cooking Time: 15 Minutes

Ingredients:

- 2 chicken breasts, boneless, skinless, flattened
- Salt and black pepper to taste
- 2 tbsp garlic powder
- 1 tsp olive oil
- 1 ½ cups mixed salad greens
- 1 tbsp red wine vinegar
- 1 cup crumbled blue cheese

Directions:

1. Season the chicken with salt, black pepper, and garlic powder. Heat oil in a pan over high heat and fry the chicken for 4 minutes on both sides until golden brown. Remove chicken to a cutting board and let cool before slicing.
2. Toss salad greens with red wine vinegar and share the salads into 4 plates. Divide chicken slices on top and sprinkle with blue cheese. Serve salad with carrots fries.

Nutrition Info:

- Info Per Servings 4g Carbs, 14g Protein, 23g Fat, 286 Calories

Tuna Salad With Lettuce & Olives

Servings: 2

Cooking Time: 5 Minutes

Ingredients:

- 1 cup canned tuna, drained
- 1 tsp onion flakes
- 3 tbsp mayonnaise
- 1 cup shredded romaine lettuce
- 1 tbsp lime juice
- Sea salt, to taste
- 6 black olives, pitted and sliced

Directions:

1. Combine the tuna, mayonnaise, lime juice, and salt in a small bowl; mix to combine well. In a salad platter, arrange the shredded lettuce and onion flakes. Spread the tuna mixture over; top with black olives to serve.

Nutrition Info:

- Info Per Servings 2g Carbs, 18.5g Protein, 20g Fat, 248 Calories

Mediterranean Salad

Servings: 4

Cooking Time: 10 Minutes

Ingredients:

- 3 tomatoes, sliced
- 1 large avocado, sliced
- 8 kalamata olives
- ¼ lb buffalo mozzarella cheese, sliced
- 2 tbsp pesto sauce
- 2 tbsp olive oil

Directions:

1. Arrange the tomato slices on a serving platter and place the avocado slices in the middle. Arrange the olives around the avocado slices and drop pieces of mozzarella on the platter. Drizzle the pesto sauce all over, and drizzle olive oil as well.

Nutrition Info:

- Info Per Servings 4.3g Carbs, 9g Protein, 25g Fat, 290 Calories

Green Salad

Servings: 4

Cooking Time: 30 Minutes

Ingredients:

- 2 cups green beans, chopped
- 2 cups shredded spinach
- ½ cup parmesan cheese
- 3 cups basil leaves
- 3 cloves of garlic
- Salt to taste
- ¼ cup olive oil

Directions:

1. Heat a little olive oil in a skillet over medium heat and add the green beans and season with salt to taste. Sauté for 3 to 5 minutes.
2. Place the green beans in a bowl and add in the spinach.
3. In a food processor, combine half of the parmesan cheese, basil, and garlic. Add in the rest of the oil and season with salt and pepper to taste.
4. Pour into the green beans and toss to coat the ingredients.

Nutrition Info:

- Info Per Servings 6g Carbs, 5g Protein, 17g Fat, 196 Calories

Clam Chowder

Servings: 5

Cooking Time: 10 Minutes

Ingredients:

- 1 can condensed cream of celery soup, undiluted
- 2 cups half-and-half cream
- 2 cans minced/chopped clams, drained
- 1/4 teaspoon ground nutmeg
- 5 tablespoons butter
- Pepper to taste

Directions:

1. In a large saucepan, combine all ingredients. Cook and stir over medium heat until heated through.

Nutrition Info:

- Info Per Servings 3.8g Carbs, 10g Protein, 14g Fat, 251 Calories

Brazilian Moqueca (shrimp Stew)

Servings: 6

Cooking Time: 25 Minutes

Ingredients:

- 1 cup coconut milk
- 2 tbsp lime juice
- ¼ cup diced roasted peppers
- 1 ½ pounds shrimp, peeled and deveined
- ¼ cup olive oil
- 1 garlic clove, minced
- 14 ounces diced tomatoes
- 2 tbsp sriracha sauce
- 1 chopped onion
- ¼ cup chopped cilantro
- Fresh dill, chopped to garnish
- Salt and black pepper, to taste

Directions:

1. Heat the olive oil in a pot over medium heat. Add onion and cook for 3 minutes or until translucent. Add the garlic and cook for another minute, until soft. Add tomatoes, shrimp, and cilantro. Cook until the shrimp becomes opaque, about 3-4 minutes.
2. Stir in sriracha sauce and coconut milk, and cook for 2 minutes. Do not bring to a boil. Stir in the lime juice and season with salt and pepper. Spoon the stew in bowls, garnish with fresh dill to serve.

Nutrition Info:

- Info Per Servings 5g Carbs, 23.1g Protein, 21g Fat, 324 Calories

Simplified French Onion Soup

Servings: 5

Cooking Time: 30 Minutes

Ingredients:

- 3 large onions, sliced
- 2 bay leaves
- 5 cups Beef Bone Broth
- 1 teaspoon dried thyme
- 1-oz Gruyere cheese, sliced into 5 equal pieces
- Pepper to taste
- 4 tablespoons oil

Directions:

1. Place a heavy-bottomed pot on medium-high fire and heat pot for 3 minutes.
2. Add oil and heat for 2 minutes. Stir in onions and sauté for 5 minutes.
3. Lower fire to medium-low, continue sautéing onions for 10 minutes until soft and browned, but not burned.
4. Add remaining ingredients and mix well.
5. Bring to a boil, lower fire to a simmer, cover and cook for 5 minutes.
6. Ladle into bowls, top with cheese.
7. Let it sit for 5 minutes.
8. Serve and enjoy.

Nutrition Info:

- Info Per Servings 9.9g Carbs, 4.3g Protein, 16.8g Fat, 208 Calories

Chicken And Cauliflower Rice Soup

Servings: 8
Cooking Time: 20 Mins
Ingredients:

- 2 cooked, boneless chicken breast halves, shredded
- 2 packages Steamed Cauliflower Rice
- 1/4 cup celery, chopped
- 1/2 cup onion, chopped
- 4 garlic cloves, minced
- Salt and ground black pepper to taste
- 2 teaspoons poultry seasoning
- 4 cups chicken broth
- ½ cup butter
- 2 cups heavy cream

Directions:

1. Heat butter in a large pot over medium heat, add onion, celery and garlic cloves to cook until tender. Meanwhile, place the riced cauliflower steam bags in the microwave following directions on the package.
2. Add the riced cauliflower, seasoning, salt and black pepper to butter mixture, saute them for 7 minutes on medium heat, stirring constantly to well combined.
3. Bring cooked chicken breast halves, broth and heavy cream to a broil. When it starts boiling, lower the heat, cover and simmer for 15 minutes.

Nutrition Info:

- Info Per Servings 6g Carbs, 27g Protein, 30g Fat, 415 Calories

Grilled Steak Salad With Pickled Peppers

Servings: 4
Cooking Time: 15 Minutes
Ingredients:

- 1 lb skirt steak, sliced
- Salt and black pepper to season
- 1 tsp olive oil
- 1 ½ cups mixed salad greens
- 3 chopped pickled peppers
- 2 tbsp red wine vinaigrette
- ½ cup crumbled queso fresco

Directions:

1. Brush the steak slices with olive oil and season with salt and pepper on both sides.
2. Heat frying pan over high heat and cook the steaks on each side to the desired doneness, for about 5-6 minutes. Remove to a bowl, cover and leave to rest while you make the salad.
3. Mix the salad greens, pickled peppers, and vinaigrette in a salad bowl. Add the beef and sprinkle with cheese. Serve the salad with roasted parsnips.

Nutrition Info:

- Info Per Servings 2g Carbs, 18g Protein, 26g Fat, 315 Calories

Brussels Sprouts Salad With Pecorino Romano

Servings: 6

Cooking Time: 35 Minutes

Ingredients:

- 2 lb Brussels sprouts, halved
- 3 tbsp olive oil
- Salt and black pepper to taste
- 2 ½ tbsp balsamic vinegar
- ¼ red cabbage, shredded
- 1 tbsp Dijon mustard
- 1 cup pecorino romano cheese, grated

Directions:

1. Preheat oven to 400ºF and line a baking sheet with foil. Toss the brussels sprouts with olive oil, a little salt, black pepper, and balsamic vinegar, in a bowl, and spread on the baking sheet in an even layer. Bake until tender on the inside and crispy on the outside, about 20 to 25 minutes.

2. Transfer to a salad bowl and add the red cabbage, Dijon mustard and half of the cheese. Mix until well combined. Sprinkle with the remaining cheese, share the salad onto serving plates, and serve with syrup-grilled salmon.

Nutrition Info:

- Info Per Servings 6g Carbs, 4g Protein, 18g Fat, 210 Calories

Kale And Brussels Sprouts

Servings: 6

Cooking Time: 0 Minutes

Ingredients:

- 1 small bunch kale, thinly sliced
- ½ pound fresh Brussels sprouts, thinly sliced
- ½ cup pistachios, chopped coarsely
- ½ cup honey mustard salad dressing
- ¼ cup parmesan cheese, shredded
- Salt and pepper to taste

Directions:

1. Place all ingredients in a salad bowl.
2. Toss to coat everything.
3. Serve.

Nutrition Info:

- Info Per Servings 9g Carbs, 5g Protein, 15g Fat, 198 Calories

Green Minestrone Soup

Servings: 4

Cooking Time: 25 Minutes

Ingredients:

- 2 tbsp ghee
- 2 tbsp onion garlic puree
- 2 heads broccoli, cut in florets
- 2 stalks celery, chopped
- 5 cups vegetable broth
- 1 cup baby spinach
- Salt and black pepper to taste

Directions:

1. Melt the ghee in a saucepan over medium heat and sauté the garlic for 3 minutes until softened. Mix in the broccoli and celery, and cook for 4 minutes until slightly tender. Pour in the broth, bring to a boil, then reduce the heat to medium-low and simmer covered for about 5 minutes.

2. Drop in the spinach to wilt, adjust the seasonings, and cook for 4 minutes. Ladle soup into serving bowls. Serve with a sprinkle of grated Gruyere cheese and freshly baked low carb carrot bread.

Nutrition Info:

- Info Per Servings 2g Carbs, 8g Protein, 20.3g Fat, 227 Calories

Asparagus Niçoise Salad

Servings: 4

Cooking Time: 0 Minutes

Ingredients:

- 1-pound fresh asparagus, trimmed and blanched
- 2 ½ ounces white tuna in oil
- ½ cup pitted Greek olives, halved
- ½ cup zesty Italian salad dressing
- Salt and pepper to taste
- 3 tablespoons olive oil

Directions:

1. Place all ingredients in a bowl.
2. Toss to mix all ingredients.
3. Serve.

Nutrition Info:

- Info Per Servings 10g Carbs, 8g Protein, 20g Fat, 239 Calories

Desserts And Drinks Recipes

Cardamom-cinnamon Spiced Coco-latte

Servings: 1
Cooking Time: 0 Minutes
Ingredients:

- ½ cup coconut milk
- ¼ tsp cardamom powder
- 1 tbsp chocolate powder
- 1 ½ cups brewed coffee, chilled
- 1 tbsp coconut oil
- ¼ tsp cinnamon
- ¼ tsp nutmeg

Directions:

1. Add all ingredients in a blender.
2. Blend until smooth and creamy.
3. Serve and enjoy.

Nutrition Info:

- Info Per Servings 7.5g Carbs, 3.8g Protein, 38.7g Fat, 362 Calories

Strawberry And Yogurt Smoothie

Servings: 3
Cooking Time: 5 Minutes
Ingredients:

- 1/2 cup yogurt
- 1 cup strawberries
- 1 teaspoon almond milk
- 1 teaspoon lime juice
- 1 1/2 teaspoons stevia

Directions:

1. Place all ingredients in a blender, blender until finely smooth. Serve and enjoy.

Nutrition Info:

- Info Per Servings 6.3g Carbs, 4.6g Protein, 12.4g Fat, 155.2 Calories

Keto Lemon Custard

Servings: 8
Cooking Time: 50 Minutes
Ingredients:

- 1 Lemon
- 6 large eggs
- 2 tbsp lemon zest
- 1 cup Lakanto
- 2 cups heavy cream

Directions:

1. Preheat oven to 300oF.
2. Mix all ingredients.
3. Pour mixture into ramekins.
4. Put ramekins into a dish with boiling water.
5. Bake in the oven for 45-50 minutes.
6. Let cool then refrigerate for 2 hours.
7. Use lemon slices as garnish.

Nutrition Info:

- Info Per Servings 4.0g Carbs, 7.0g Protein, 21.0g Fat, 233 Calories

Dark Chocolate Mousse With Stewed Plums

Servings: 6
Cooking Time: 45 Minutes
Ingredients:

- 12 oz unsweetened chocolate
- 8 eggs, separated into yolks and whites
- 2 tbsp salt
- ¾ cup swerve sugar
- ½ cup olive oil
- 3 tbsp brewed coffee
- Stewed Plums
- 4 plums, pitted and halved
- ½ stick cinnamon
- ½ cup swerve
- ½ cup water
- ½ lemon, juiced

Directions:

1. Put the chocolate in a bowl and melt in the microwave for 1 ½ minutes. In a separate bowl, whisk the yolks with half of the swerve until a pale yellow has formed, then, beat in the salt, olive oil, and coffee. Mix in the melted chocolate until smooth.
2. In a third bowl, whisk the whites with the hand mixer until a soft peak has formed. Sprinkle the remaining swerve sugar over and gently fold in with a spatula. Fetch a tablespoon full of the chocolate mixture and fold in to combine. Pour in the remaining chocolate mixture and whisk to mix.
3. Pour the mousse into 6 ramekins, cover with plastic wrap, and refrigerate overnight. The next morning, pour water, swerve, cinnamon, and lemon juice in a saucepan and bring to a simmer for 3 minutes, occasionally stirring to ensure the swerve has dissolved and a syrup has formed.
4. Add the plums and poach in the sweetened water for 18 minutes until soft. Turn the heat off and discard the cinnamon stick. Spoon a plum each with syrup on the chocolate mousse and serve.

Nutrition Info:

- Info Per Servings 6.9g Carbs, 9.5g Protein, 23g Fat, 288 Calories

Coconut-mocha Shake

Servings: 1
Cooking Time: 0 Minutes
Ingredients:

- 2 tbsp cocoa powder
- 1 tbsp coconut flakes, unsweetened
- 2 packet Stevia, or more to taste
- 1 cup brewed coffee, chilled
- 3 tbsps coconut oil

Directions:

1. Add all ingredients in a blender.
2. Blend until smooth and creamy.
3. Serve and enjoy.

Nutrition Info:

- Info Per Servings 9g Carbs, 2.4g Protein, 43.7g Fat, 402 Calories

Crispy Zucchini Chips

Servings: 5

Cooking Time: 20 Mins

Ingredients:

- 1 large egg, beaten
- 1 cup. almond flour
- 1 medium zucchini, thinly sliced
- 3/4 cup Parmesan cheese, grated
- Cooking spray

Directions:

1. Preheat oven to 400 degrees F. Line a baking pan with parchment paper.
2. In a bowl, mix together Parmesan cheese and almond flour.
3. In another bowl whisk the egg. Dip each zucchini slice in the egg, then the cheese mixture until finely coated.
4. Spray zucchini slices with cooking spray and place in the prepared oven.
5. Bake for 20 minutes until crispy. Serve.

Nutrition Info:

- Info Per Servings 16.8g Carbs, 10.8g Protein, 6g Fat, 215.2 Calories

Garden Greens & Yogurt Shake

Servings: 1

Cooking Time: 0 Minutes

Ingredients:

- 1 cup whole milk yogurt
- 1 cup Garden greens
- 3 tbsp MCT oil
- 1 tbsp flaxseed, ground
- 1 cup water
- 1 packet Stevia, or more to taste

Directions:

1. Add all ingredients in a blender.
2. Blend until smooth and creamy.
3. Serve and enjoy.

Nutrition Info:

- Info Per Servings 7.2g Carbs, 11.7g Protein, 53g Fat, 581 Calories

Strawberry Yogurt Shake

Servings: 1

Cooking Time: 0 Minutes

Ingredients:

- ½ cup whole milk yogurt
- 4 strawberries, chopped
- 1 tbsp cocoa powder
- 3 tbsp coconut oil
- 1 tbsp pepitas
- 1 ½ cups water
- 1 packet Stevia, or more to taste

Directions:

1. Add all ingredients in a blender.
2. Blend until smooth and creamy.
3. Serve and enjoy.

Nutrition Info:

- Info Per Servings 10.5g Carbs, 7.7g Protein, 49.3g Fat, 496 Calories

Cranberry White Chocolate Barks

Servings: 6

Cooking Time: 5 Minutes

Ingredients:

- 10 oz unsweetened white chocolate, chopped
- ½ cup erythritol
- ⅓ cup dried cranberries, chopped
- ⅓ cup toasted walnuts, chopped
- ¼ tsp pink salt

Directions:

1. Line a baking sheet with parchment paper. Pour chocolate and erythritol in a bowl, and melt in the microwave for 25 seconds, stirring three times until fully melted. Stir in the cranberries, walnuts, and salt, reserving a few cranberries and walnuts for garnishing.
2. Pour the mixture on the baking sheet and spread out. Sprinkle with remaining cranberries and walnuts. Refrigerate for 2 hours to set. Break into bite-size pieces to serve.

Nutrition Info:

- Info Per Servings 3g Carbs, 6g Protein, 21g Fat, 225 Calories

No Nuts Fudge

Servings: 15

Cooking Time: 4 Hours

Ingredients:

- ¼ cup cocoa powder
- ½ teaspoon baking powder
- 1 stick of butter, melted
- 4 tablespoons erythritol
- 6 eggs, beaten
- Salt to taste.

Directions:

1. Mix all ingredients in a slow cooker.
2. Add a pinch of salt.
3. Mix until well combined.
4. Cover pot.
5. Press the low settings and adjust the time to 4 hours.

Nutrition Info:

- Info Per Servings 1.3g Carbs, 4.3g Protein, 12.2g Fat, 132 Calories

Minty-coco And Greens Shake

Servings: 1

Cooking Time: 0 Minutes

Ingredients:

- ½ cup coconut milk
- 2 peppermint leaves
- 2 packets Stevia, or as needed
- 1 cup 50/50 salad mix
- 1 tbsp coconut oil
- 1 ½ cups water

Directions:

1. Add all ingredients in a blender.
2. Blend until smooth and creamy.
3. Serve and enjoy.

Nutrition Info:

- Info Per Servings 5.8g Carbs, 2.7g Protein, 37.8g Fat, 344 Calories

Eggnog Keto Custard

Servings: 8

Cooking Time: 10 Minutes

Ingredients:

- ¼ tsp nutmeg
- ¼ Truvia
- ½ cup heavy whipping cream
- 1 cup half and half
- 4 eggs

Directions:

1. Blend all ingredients together.
2. Pour evenly into 6 ramekins (microwave safe).
3. Microwave at 50% power for 4 minutes then stir thoroughly.
4. Microwave for another 3-4 minutes at 50% power then stir well again.
5. Serve either cool or hot.

Nutrition Info:

- Info Per Servings 1.0g Carbs, 3.0g Protein, 6.0g Fat, 70 Calories

Almond Butter Fat Bombs

Servings: 4

Cooking Time: 3 Minutes + Cooling Time

Ingredients:

- ½ cup almond butter
- ½ cup coconut oil
- 4 tbsp unsweetened cocoa powder
- ½ cup erythritol

Directions:

1. Melt butter and coconut oil in the microwave for 45 seconds, stirring twice until properly melted and mixed. Mix in cocoa powder and erythritol until completely combined.
2. Pour into muffin moulds and refrigerate for 3 hours to harden.

Nutrition Info:

- Info Per Servings 2g Carbs, 4g Protein, 18.3g Fat, 193 Calories

Chocolate Bark With Almonds

Servings: 12

Cooking Time: 1 Hour 15 Minutes

Ingredients:

- ½ cup toasted almonds, chopped
- ½ cup butter
- 10 drops stevia
- ¼ tsp salt
- ½ cup unsweetened coconut flakes
- 4 ounces dark chocolate

Directions:

1. Melt together the butter and chocolate, in the microwave, for 90 seconds. Remove and stir in stevia.
2. Line a cookie sheet with waxed paper and spread the chocolate evenly. Scatter the almonds on top, coconut flakes, and sprinkle with salt. Refrigerate for one hour.

Nutrition Info:

- Info Per Servings 1.9g Carbs, 1.9g Protein, 15.3g Fat, 161 Calories

Spicy Cheese Crackers

Servings: 4

Cooking Time: 10 Mins

Ingredients:

- 3/4 cup almond flour
- 1 egg
- 2 tablespoons cream cheese
- 2 cups shredded Parmesan cheese
- 1/2 teaspoon red pepper flakes
- 1 tablespoon dry ranch salad dressing mix

Directions:

1. Preheat oven to 425 degrees F.
2. Combine Parmesan and cream cheese in a microwave safe bowl and microwave in 30 second intervals. Add the cheese to mix well, and whisk along the almond flour, egg, ranch seasoning, and red pepper flakes, stirring occasionally.
3. Transfer the dough in between two parchment-lined baking sheets. Form the dough into rolls by cutting off plum-sized pieces of dough with dough cutter into 1-inch square pieces, yielding about 60 pieces.
4. Place crackers to a baking sheet lined parchment. Bake for 5 minutes, flipping halfway, then continue to bake for 5 minutes more. Chill before serving.

Nutrition Info:

- Info Per Servings 18g Carbs, 17g Protein, 4g Fat, 235 Calories

Vanilla Jello Keto Way

Servings: 6

Cooking Time: 6 Minutes

Ingredients:

- 1 cup heavy cream
- 1 teaspoon vanilla extract
- 2 tablespoons gelatin powder, unsweetened
- 3 tablespoons erythritol
- 1 cup boiling water

Directions:

1. Place the boiling water in a small pot and bring to a simmer.
2. Add the gelatin powder and allow to dissolve.
3. Stir in the rest of the ingredients.
4. Pour the mixture into jello molds.
5. Place in the fridge to set for 2 hours.

Nutrition Info:

- Info Per Servings 5.2g Carbs, 3.3g Protein, 7.9g Fat, 105 Calories

Sea Salt 'n Macadamia Choco Barks

Servings: 10
Cooking Time: 5 Minutes
Ingredients:

- 1 teaspoon sea salt flakes
- 1/4 cup macadamia nuts, crushed
- 2 Tablespoons erythritol or stevia, to taste
- 3.5 oz 100% dark chocolate, broken into pieces
- 2 Tablespoons coconut oil, melted

Directions:

1. Melt the chocolate and coconut oil over a very low heat.
2. Remove from heat. Stir in sweetener.
3. Pour the mixture into a loaf pan and place in the fridge for 15 minutes.
4. Scatter the crushed macadamia nuts on top along with the sea salt. Lightly press into the chocolate.
5. Place back into the fridge or freezer for 2 hours.

Nutrition Info:

- Info Per Servings 1.0g Carbs, 2.0g Protein, 8.0g Fat, 84 Calories

Lemon Gummies

Servings: 4
Cooking Time: 15 Minutes
Ingredients:

- 1/4 cup fresh lemon juice
- 2 Tablespoons gelatin powder
- 2 Tablespoons stevia, to taste
- ½ cup half and half
- 1 Tablespoon water

Directions:

1. In a small saucepan, heat up water and lemon juice.
2. Slowly stir in the gelatin powder and the rest of the ingredients. Heating and mixing well until dissolved.
3. Pour into silicone molds.
4. Freeze or refrigerate for 2+ hours until firm.

Nutrition Info:

- Info Per Servings 1.0g Carbs, 3.0g Protein, 7g Fat, 88 Calories

Strawberry-coconut Shake

Servings: 1
Cooking Time: 0 Minutes
Ingredients:

- ½ cup whole milk yogurt
- 3 tbsp MCT oil
- ¼ cup strawberries, chopped
- 1 tbsp coconut flakes, unsweetened
- 1 tbsp hemp seeds
- 1 ½ cups water
- 1 packet Stevia, or more to taste

Directions:

1. Add all ingredients in a blender.
2. Blend until smooth and creamy.
3. Serve and enjoy.

Nutrition Info:

- Info Per Servings 10.2g Carbs, 6.4g Protein, 50.9g Fat, 511 Calories

Cream Cheese 'n Coconut Cookies

Servings: 15

Cooking Time: 17 Minutes

Ingredients:

- 1 Egg
- 1/2 cup Butter softened
- 1/2 cup Coconut Flour
- 1/2 cup Erythritol or other sugar substitutes
- 3 tablespoons Cream cheese, softened
- 1 teaspoon Vanilla extract
- 1/4 teaspoon salt
- 1/2 teaspoon baking powder

Directions:

1. In a mixing bowl, whisk well erythritol, cream cheese, and butter.
2. Add egg and vanilla. Beat until thoroughly combined.
3. Mix in salt, baking powder, and coconut flour.
4. On an 11x13-inch piece of wax paper, place the batter. Mold into a log shape and then twist the ends to secure. Refrigerate for an hour and then slice into 1-inch circles.
5. When ready, preheat oven to 350oF and line a baking sheet with foil. Place cookies at least 1/2-inch apart.
6. Pop in the oven and bake until golden brown, around 17 minutes.
7. Serve and enjoy.

Nutrition Info:

- Info Per Servings 3.0g Carbs, 1.0g Protein, 8.0g Fat, 88 Calories

Chocolate Cakes

Servings: 6

Cooking Time: 25 Minutes

Ingredients:

- ½ cup almond flour
- ¼ cup xylitol
- 1 tsp baking powder
- ½ tsp baking soda
- 1 tsp cinnamon, ground
- A pinch of salt
- A pinch of ground cloves
- ½ cup butter, melted
- ½ cup buttermilk
- 1 egg
- 1 tsp pure almond extract
- For the Frosting:
- 1 cup double cream
- 1 cup dark chocolate, flaked

Directions:

1. Preheat the oven to 360ºF. Use a cooking spray to grease a donut pan.
2. In a bowl, mix the cloves, almond flour, baking powder, salt, baking soda, xylitol, and cinnamon. In a separate bowl, combine the almond extract, butter, egg, buttermilk, and cream. Mix the wet mixture into the dry mixture. Evenly ladle the batter into the donut pan. Bake for 17 minutes.
3. Set a pan over medium heat and warm double cream; simmer for 2 minutes. Fold in the chocolate flakes; combine until all the chocolate melts; let cool. Spread the top of the cakes with the frosting.

Nutrition Info:

- Info Per Servings 10g Carbs, 4.8g Protein, 20g Fat, 218 Calories

Chocolate Hazelnut Bites

Servings: 9

Cooking Time: 0 Minutes

Ingredients:

- 1 carton spreadable cream cheese
- 1 cup semisweet chocolate chips, melted
- 1/2 cup Nutella
- 2-1/4 cups graham cracker crumbs
- 2 cups chopped hazelnuts, toasted
- 5 tablespoons butter

Directions:

1. Beat cream cheese, melted chocolate chips, and Nutella until blended. Stir in cracker crumbs. Refrigerate until firm enough to roll, about 30 minutes.
2. Shape mixture into 1-in. balls; roll in chopped hazelnuts. Make an indentation in the center of each with the end of a wooden spoon handle. Fill with a hazelnut. Store between layers of waxed paper in an airtight container in the refrigerator.

Nutrition Info:

- Info Per Servings 10g Carbs, 2.7g Protein, 14g Fat, 176 Calories

Chia And Blackberry Pudding

Servings: 2

Cooking Time: 10 Minutes

Ingredients:

- 1 cup full-fat natural yogurt
- 2 tsp swerve
- 2 tbsp chia seeds
- 1 cup fresh blackberries
- 1 tbsp lemon zest
- Mint leaves, to serve

Directions:

1. Mix together the yogurt and the swerve. Stir in the chia seeds. Reserve 4 blackberries for garnish and mash the remaining ones with a fork until pureed. Stir in the yogurt mixture
2. Chill in the fridge for 30 minutes. When cooled, divide the mixture between 2 glasses. Top each with a couple of raspberries, mint leaves, lemon zest and serve.

Nutrition Info:

- Info Per Servings 4.7g Carbs, 7.5g Protein, 10g Fat, 169 Calories

Raspberry Creamy Smoothie

Servings: 1

Cooking Time: 0 Minutes

Ingredients:

- ¼ cup coconut milk
- 1 ½ cups brewed coffee, chilled
- 2 tbsps raspberries
- 2 tbsps avocado meat
- 1 tsp chia seeds
- 2 packets Stevia or more to taste
- 3 tbsps coconut oil

Directions:

1. Add all ingredients in a blender.
2. Blend until smooth and creamy.
3. Serve and enjoy.

Nutrition Info:

- Info Per Servings 8.2g Carbs, 4.9g Protein, 33.2g Fat, 350 Calories

Granny Smith Apple Tart

Servings: 8
Cooking Time: 65 Minutes
Ingredients:

- 6 tbsp butter
- 2 cups almond flour
- 1 tsp cinnamon
- ⅓ cup sweetener
- Filling:
- 2 cups sliced Granny Smith
- ¼ cup butter

- ¼ cup sweetener
- ½ tsp cinnamon
- ½ tsp lemon juice
- Topping:
- ¼ tsp cinnamon
- 2 tbsp sweetener

Directions:

1. Preheat your oven to 370°F and combine all crust ingredients in a bowl. Press this mixture into the bottom of a greased pan. Bake for 5 minutes.
2. Meanwhile, combine the apples and lemon juice in a bowl and let them sit until the crust is ready. Arrange them on top of the crust. Combine the rest of the filling ingredients, and brush this mixture over the apples. Bake for about 30 minutes.
3. Press the apples down with a spatula, return to oven, and bake for 20 more minutes. Combine the cinnamon and sweetener, in a bowl, and sprinkle over the tart.
4. Note: Granny Smith apples have just 9.5g of net carbs per 100g. Still high for you? Substitute with Chayote squash, which has the same texture and rich nutrients, and just around 4g of net carbs .

Nutrition Info:

- Info Per Servings 6.7g Carbs, 7g Protein, 26g Fat, 302 Calories

Chocolate Marshmallows

Servings: 4
Cooking Time: 30 Minutes
Ingredients:

- 2 tbsp unsweetened cocoa powder
- ½ tsp vanilla extract
- ½ cup swerve
- 1 tbsp xanthan gum mixed in 1 tbsp water
- A pinch Salt

- 6 tbsp Cool water
- 2 ½ tsp Gelatin powder
- Dusting:
- 1 tbsp unsweetened cocoa powder
- 1 tbsp swerve confectioner's sugar

Directions:

1. Line the loaf pan with parchment paper and grease with cooking spray; set aside. In a saucepan, mix the swerve, 2 tbsp of water, xanthan gum mixture, and salt. Place the pan over medium heat and bring to a boil. Insert the thermometer and let the ingredients simmer to 238 F, for 7 minutes.
2. In a small bowl, add 2 tbsp of water and sprinkle the gelatin on top. Let sit there without stirring to dissolve for 5 minutes. While the gelatin dissolves, pour the remaining water in a small bowl and heat in the microwave for 30 seconds. Stir in cocoa powder and mix it into the gelatin.
3. When the sugar solution has hit the right temperature, gradually pour it directly into the gelatin mixture while continuously whisking. Beat for 10 minutes to get a light and fluffy consistency.
4. Next, stir in the vanilla and pour the blend into the loaf pan. Let the marshmallows set for 3 hours and then use an oiled knife to cut it into cubes; place them on a plate. Mix the remaining cocoa powder and confectioner's sugar together. Sift it over the marshmallows.

Nutrition Info:

- Info Per Servings 5.1g Carbs, 0.5g Protein, 2.2g Fat, 55 Calories

Appendix : Recipes Index

G

Garden Greens & Yogurt Shake 73
Garlic & Ginger Chicken With Peanut Sauce 26
Garlic And Basil Mashed Celeriac 14
Garlic Chicken Salad 65
Garlic Flavored Kale Taters 9
Garlic Lime Marinated Pork Chops 32
Garlic Pork Chops With Mint Pesto 37
Garlicky Cheddar Biscuits 13
Granny Smith Apple Tart 80
Green Minestrone Soup 70
Green Salad 66
Green Salad With Bacon And Blue Cheese 61
Grilled Cheese The Keto Way 58
Grilled Lamb On Lemony Sauce 28
Grilled Parmesan Eggplant 55
Grilled Shrimp With Chimichurri Sauce 42
Grilled Sirloin Steak With Sauce Diane 36
Grilled Spicy Eggplant 54
Grilled Steak Salad With Pickled Peppers 68

H

Habanero Chicken Wings 16
Halibut En Papillote 44
Herb Butter With Parsley 52
Herbed Portobello Mushrooms 56
Herby Chicken Meatballs 21
Homemade Classic Beef Burgers 30

K

Kale And Brussels Sprouts 69
Keto Lemon Custard 71
Keto-approved Trail Mix 12

L

Lamb Stew With Veggies 38
Lemon Cauliflower "couscous" With Halloumi 59
Lemon Chili Halibut 45
Lemon Garlic Shrimp 47
Lemon Gummies 77

M

Mediterranean Salad 66
Minty-coco And Greens Shake 74
Morning Coconut Smoothie 58
Mushroom Soup 60

N

New York Strip Steak With Mushroom Sauce 34
No Nuts Fudge 74
Nutty Avocado Crostini With Nori 10

O

One-pot Chicken With Mushrooms And Spinach 24
Onion & Nuts Stuffed Mushrooms 57

P

Parmesan Crackers 7
Parmesan Fish Bake 39
Parmesan Roasted Cabbage 50
Parmesan Wings With Yogurt Sauce 19
Parsnip And Carrot Fries With Aioli 8
Parsnip Chips With Avocado Dip 51
Pesto Chicken 20
Pistachio-crusted Salmon 40
Pork Burgers With Caramelized Onion Rings 27
Pork Chops With Cranberry Sauce 27
Pork Osso Bucco 30
Pumpkin & Meat Peanut Stew 62
Pumpkin Bake 57

Q

Quail Eggs And Winter Melon Soup 65

R

Raspberry Creamy Smoothie 79
Red Cabbage Tilapia Taco Bowl 47
Ricotta And Pomegranate 6
Russian Beef Gratin 28

S

Salmon Panzanella 41
Sautéed Celeriac With Tomato Sauce 54
Sea Salt 'n Macadamia Choco Barks 77
Seared Scallops With Chorizo And Asiago Cheese 44
Seasoned Salmon With Parmesan 40
Shrimp Fra Diavolo 12
Shrimp With Avocado & Cauliflower Salad 64
Simple Beef Curry 33
Simple Steamed Salmon Fillets 46
Simple Tender Crisp Cauli-bites 12
Simplified French Onion Soup 67

Simply Steamed Alaskan Cod 49
Smoky Baby Back Ribs 37
Sour Cream Salmon With Parmesan 41
Spanish Chicken 18
Spiced Baked Pork With Milk 29
Spicy Cheese Crackers 76
Spinach Artichoke Heart Chicken 22
Steamed Cod With Ginger 40
Steamed Herbed Red Snapper 48
Stewed Chicken Salsa 23
Stewed Italian Chicken 16
Strawberry And Yogurt Smoothie 71
Strawberry Mug Cake 57
Strawberry Yogurt Shake 73
Strawberry-coconut Shake 77
Stuffed Avocados With Chicken 23
Stuffed Jalapeno 15

T

Tasty Cauliflower Dip 56
Thyme Chicken Thighs 26
Thyme-sesame Crusted Halibut 42
Traditional Greek Salad 60
Tuna Salad With Lettuce & Olives 65
Tuna Topped Pickles 7
Turkey Fajitas 18

V

Vanilla Jello Keto Way 76
Vegan Mushroom Pizza 52

W

Walnut Butter On Cracker 6
Watermelon And Cucumber Salad 60

Y

Yummy Chicken Nuggets 16
Yummy Shrimp Fried Rice 39

Z

Zoodles With Avocado & Olives 59
Zucchini Noodles 53
Zucchini Spaghetti With Turkey Bolognese Sauce 22

Printed in Great Britain
by Amazon

28488632R00053